DARE TO BE AN EAGLE

Gill Gifford

2008

First Edition

Published and Printed by

Leiston Press
Masterlord Industrial Estate
Leiston
Suffolk
IP16 4JD
Telephone Number: 01728 833003
Email: glenn@leistonpress.com

ISBN 978-0-9554725-8-9

Acknowledgements

First of all, there are simply no words to convey my complete gratitude to my Heavenly Father, the Beloved Lord Jesus and my friend The Holy Spirit. When I fell in love with my Saviour on that day in December 1979 it became my quest to know the Holy Spirit as Lord more and more. He has been so faithful, even when I let Him down, He never let go of my hand! As long as I live, I will be eternally grateful and acknowledge that all Glory and Honour is due to Him.

Then there is my dearest husband Skippy, what can I say? He has never ceased over the years to encourage me, believe in me and release me to fulfil the call on my life. Darling I love you and appreciate you. Thank you with all my heart for every word of wisdom and support you have always given me, I would not have been able to complete this book if you had not unselfishly given up our times together. Your reward is awaiting you in heaven!

To my family, I love you, you are such a blessing and one day you will realize just how much you mean to me. It is a "forever prayer" that our children and our children's children are blessed to a thousand generations. Thank you for honouring Skippy and I as your parents and grandparents, even though we messed it up so often! To my adopted son, Isaac in Kampala, you have been a real blessing to me, thank you for all your prayers. May all of you always know the love of The Father and continue to grow in His Grace day by day.

Then there are you very special people who **"believed"** in me and I know without your input in my life I would never be where I am today. You took a risk and released me to minister and I just want to say a real heartfelt thank you to Rachel Hickson and Don Double especially. Dare to be an Eagle was conceived in my spirit many years ago and one day in heaven I will be able to tell Bob Gordon personally just how appreciative I am for his teaching and discipleship I received during my time as a Student at Roffey Place. Now, as I am blessed with my own Team, I am only too aware that my example is paramount and it is such a privilege to **"believe"** in others and see them begin to soar! Thank you to each of you who serve me so wonderfully, as Skippy always says, "Gill, you could never do it without them," how true! Certainly this book would not have got this far without the work of Susie, bless you so much.

Many, who know me well, will understand the overwhelming longing I have at many times to be with the Lord, the foretaste of heaven has left a mark on my life and inspired me to "press toward the goal."[but not one day before the Lord calls me home!] I want to acknowledge this has been the motivation of my life to "please" my Father God and my desire is that I leave this legacy for others after me.

CONTENTS

Foreword

Dare to be an Eagle

I have known Gill now for almost 30 years and right from the day I met her, I knew she was a woman who goes 'all out' for God. It has been thrilling and challenging to watch Gill's spiritual journey thus far – no half-measures, shortcuts or compromise, but eyes fixed on Jesus all the way.

1 Corinthians 15:46 says, "First the natural, then the spiritual." The Scriptures take many illustrations from nature to demonstrate a spiritual principle. "Why do you worry about clothing? Consider the lilies of the field … look at the birds of the air … your heavenly Father feeds them." (Matt 6:28) "Go to the ant, thou sluggard, consider her ways and be wise."(Prov 6:6) And here we have the eagle – what a magnificent bird! Gill has researched well the ways of the eagle and drawn out some superb spiritual lessons.

I heard a story of a man looking around a zoo and when he got to the bird enclosure, he stood outside and looked at an eagle on a perch and wept. There was this incredible bird, made for the skies, but imprisoned in a cage.

We're not chickens, scratching around for food and earthbound, but eagles – created to soar high into the presence of God. I love the principle that the eagle needs to feed on 'live meat', just as we need to live on the fresh Word of God, not handouts. Good as CDs, DVDs and sermons are, we must soar like the eagle and feed directly from the 'Bread of Life'.

It is so good that Gill stops frequently and encourages us to pray, to confirm and make good the different principles as we go through the book; by the end it was as if she had literally been changed from "one degree of glory to another, into the very likeness of Christ", and so can we.

Hilda Gordon
Author of 'I'll Walk with God'

i

There are always seasons of life when we are challenged to risk and jump! A good friend of mine always says - "You never know, unless you have a go." Although this is true it is not always so easy to let go and jump. So often our past does limit our future and so we need a fresh vision of who we are and what God can do! In this book Gill Gifford describes the process of letting go and letting God teach you to fly again into all your purpose and destiny. Gill is a passionate communicator who takes scripture and helps you renew your focus and through prayer and new insights alters your way of thinking. This book will encourage you to FLY once again!

Rachel Hickson
Heartcry Ministries, Director & Founder.

Author of 2 books - Supernatural Communication and Supernatural Breakthrough.

Gilly is truly a "Woman of the Word"!! I have known her and ministered with her over the past 15years and the principles she has presented in "Dare to be an Eagle" are the very fabric of her own personal life and teaching. Her passion for Jesus to be raised up and glorified,whatever may be happening around her is always the motivating principle underlying her ministry. Dare to pick up and read this book! Dare to be encouraged and revitalised afresh! I urge you to read it...then follow the flight path she lays out....and find **yourself** soaring as an eagle; thrilling at the joy of serving our Lord Jesus on your new flight path. This book will call you to "come up higher, come ever closer to God." You will, I know, find yourself urging others to read it themselves.

Maureen Howe
Eastbourne.

Introduction

"Oh Lord please don't let me miss anything you want to give me!"

There are times in our Christian journey when we are just not expecting anything and yet, suddenly, the Spirit of God bursts through so unexpectedly that it sends shock waves to the very core of our being and at the same time sets off a series of "domino effects" in our lives that shake us for a moment. It is as if heaven breaks through and revelation cascades at the speed of light into our spirit. How may we capture what is so elusive, so precious and so dynamic?

"Oh Lord please don't let me miss anything you want to give me!"

It was one of those moments as I sat down with my two grandsons several years ago to watch one of their Video Cartoons. "You'll like it Nana!" they excitedly exclaimed. "It's not nasty, it's lovely!" How the boys love to protect me in selecting what I should or shouldn't watch! So I settled down to watch "Rescuers Down Under" never imagining what the Holy Spirit had in store that would change my life forever. The story is of a young boy who loves the wild life in the Out-Back in Australia and the video starts with him looking through his binoculars when he suddenly sees a beautiful eagle caught in a vicious trap on an enormous rock screeching for help. It was at this particular moment, that my spirit was suddenly quickened and my spiritual eyes opened. I heard the sound of weeping and found myself weeping uncontrollably just as it is in **Rev 5:4** *"I wept audibly because no one was found fit to open the scroll."* In an instant I knew that the Lord was whispering to me that I was witnessing the heartbreak He felt when He looked at so many in the Church. Yes, they were Born Again and believed in Jesus; yes they were Re-Created in Him but instead of living the unlimited, fearless lives as spiritual eagles, they were caught in a trap, even though they had been planted on the Rock Christ Jesus. It was as if The Spirit was calling me to be one of His channels of "liberation" to His people. In fact the young lad immediately responded setting off with just his knife. He never for a moment hesitated or even considered his own inadequacy; he was completely focused on liberating the trapped eagle! No, it wasn't easy. At first the eagle fought against the boy as he was full of fear and even flipped him off the high rock to an almost certain death. The liberated eagle then realized that he was free and swooped down to rescue him. So began a love-relationship and a journey of intimacy between the eagle and the boy. As I wept I knew I couldn't just sit still and ignore the cries for help coming from God's children.

FREEDOM is our inheritance and we are always called to be free and then to give away that freedom to others. After all, wasn't that what Jesus came to do: *"The Spirit of The Lord is upon Me, because He has anointed Me to preach the good news to the poor; He has sent Me to announce release to the captives and recovery of sight to the blind, to send forth as delivered those who are oppressed, who are downtrodden, bruised, crushed, and broken down by calamity: To proclaim the acceptable year of The Lord."* **Luke 4:18.**

That unexpected day something was born in my spirit-man and I began to research, to seek out, and long for all possible information about eagles, their habits, their lives and especially what the Bible had to tell me about these wonderful birds. I found that I had so much to learn, so much to apply spiritually that now I just want to bless you and share my journey with you. I am indebted to the books that have been written, and also to the people who have preached about "Soaring with Eagles Wings" such as Joyce Meyer. I am so grateful for their inspiration that has kept me "digging" for gold!

Dare to be an Eagle was born that day, but it has taken years to draw out the treasures which I pray will build you up, encourage you and inspire you to live out an intimate Spirit-filled life of unlimited horizons and move you towards your own destiny, to the Glory of Jesus.

Chapter 1

THE DIVINE EAGLE

"He found him in a desert land, in the howling void of the wilderness; He kept circling around him, He scanned him penetratingly. He kept him as the pupil of His eye. ___As an eagle___ *that stirs up her nest that flutters over her young, He spread abroad His wings and He took them, He bore them on His pinions."* **Deut 32:1-14**

The Divine Eagle is where God is pictured as The Great Almighty God of the Universe. Moses tells us about this in: **Deut 32: 2-4** *"My message shall drop as the rain, my speech shall distil as the dew.....to proclaim the Name and the Presence of the Lord. To ascribe greatness to our God, He is the Rock, His work is perfect, for all His ways are law and justice. A God of faithfulness."* BUT He goes on to say that: *"His own people, Israel, have spoiled themselves by not being sons to Him.* Here we see in verse 6 one of the few times in the Old Testament where God is speaking from His Father heart: *"Is not He your Father Who acquired you for His own?"* and Verse 9 *"For The Lord's portion is His people"* and Verse 10 *"And He found them."*

Moses ran out of words saying, *"**As an eagle...He found them.**"*

"All His ways" proclaim Who God is; His insurmountable greatness; His utter perfection; His everlasting faithfulness and unparalleled love......this is **WHO HE IS**.....so with the eagle, all his ways reflect even more of the mysteries of God.

My Divine Eagle is God Himself, and He found me! Some may believe that they have found Him, but the truth is He always was the Good Shepherd who looked for His lost sheep. Long before we knew we needed Him, He was looking for us and He came seeking those who would respond to His

1

love and BE FOUND by Him!

I was forty years old and it had been a long hard wilderness. Much of it, I have to say, was of my own making. Doing what "I" want is sin and is the root of all rebellion and brings its own consequences. Sometimes it might seem good, but only for a season; inevitably it has a sting in the tail which brings heartache, pain and brokenness to you and others. Rebellion and Rejection stem from the same root, the Fall of Man in the Garden of Eden, when Adam and Eve chose not to listen to God's command not to eat of the fruit of that particular tree. God never intended for mankind to have the knowledge of good and evil, but they did what they wanted, and it resulted in the loss of relationship with God, for them, and all of mankind that followed.

My parents tried to give me good advice not to marry a particular man, but in my rebellion, like Adam and Eve, I made a bad choice and it led me into fifteen years of abuse - and all I could think was that it was my fault. All of us have to blame someone; many blame God or other people, or like me, blamed myself. **Genesis 3:12** Adam blamed God, *"it was the woman You gave me"*, and then Eve blamed the serpent and ever since, mankind has been playing the "Blame Game"......" it's not my fault; it's my father, my mother, my family, my children, my teacher, my employer, my past, my lack of finances, my circumstances etc etc!" So here we see that Moses is reminding the Israelites, God's chosen people, that He had found them..... *"As an eagle that stirs up her nest and flutters over her young. He spread abroad His wings and He took them, He bore them on His pinions"* So the Lord alone led them."

If you have studied the ways of an eagle you will know that the eagle has unparalleled eye sight amongst all of God's creation. He can see a small coin in tall grass from as far up as three miles in the sky. He also has a width of vision for at least fifty miles! God, as our Divine Eagle, is always able to see us. He saw us in the past, He sees us in the present and also in the future.....He knows our pain, our heartache and every circumstance in our lives. During those fifteen years, I would often cry out, "God where are you?" The truth was He was already there, but I was not ready to welcome Him as my Divine Eagle and allow Him to find me.

An example of this can be found in **Matthew 14:22-33.** The Disciples had been obedient to Jesus and got into the boat to go to the other side of the lake; they had even allowed Jesus to take care of the crowds! We, too, need to allow Jesus to deal with all the things that crowd in on our lives: the pressures, the circumstances, our past experiences and even our own feelings about ourselves! We need to let Jesus dismiss the crowds! The Disciples were doing so well, but then a STORM came from seemingly nowhere. It was dark and they could not see Jesus. They were struggling in their own strength, rowing as hard as they could, and yet the wind was against them. They were many miles from the shore fighting the heavy waves, desperately vulnerable, fearful, panicking and getting nowhere fast! "Where was Jesus?" "Didn't He care?" But you know Jesus could see them all the time, even from up in the hills where He was praying. He came to them **walking upon their very problem!** All the Disciples wanted was Jesus, but they didn't expect Him to come like that, so they didn't recognise Him....they thought He was a ghost! Fear makes us imagine all sorts of things! But what I want you to see, is that no matter what circumstances are, even when we feel that we have been abandoned, or our thoughts are telling us that He doesn't care....**Its a lie!** He is The Divine Eagle and He sees exactly where we are, He knows exactly how He will come to our rescue and how He will "find" us in whatever is our crisis situation. **HE WILL COME!** He will bring with Him: **courage, comfort** and even **confrontation of our fears** and **draw us to Himself** even if it means walking on the water! It could be that there are things crowding into your life right now or you may wonder if the Lord really cares about you; why don't you put these things into the hands of the Holy Spirit?

Father, I come to You now, in the Name of the Lord Jesus Christ, please will You to take care of all the things and pressures that are crowding into my life. I confess that sometimes I even feel as if You don't care. I recognize that this is a lie from satan, please forgive me Lord, I need Your help Holy Spirit....especially as I read this book, so that I will not miss what You are going to say to me. Thank You Father. Amen.

So, even in my years of wilderness, of utter despair and fear, The Divine Eagle was watching over me, patiently waiting for me to be ready to respond to Him. During those years He always had a "well of living water" for me to drink from, like Hagar in **Genesis 21:19** *"Then God opened her eyes and she saw a well of water; and filled the empty water bottle with water and caused the youth to drink."* Abraham had just sent Hagar and her son away and we are told, *"She wandered aimlessly and lost her way in the wilderness of Beersheba."* How easy it is for us to do the same; wandering aimlessly and losing our way, even as Christians! Help us Lord! Praise God, in her hour of need, we are told that, *"God heard her and the angel of God called out to Hagar from heaven. What troubles you Hagar? Fear not, for God has heard .....ARISE!"* May be today the Holy Spirit is saying that to you, "ARISE from your despair, arise from your self-pity, arise from all those negative thoughts about yourself and drink from the well of living water and He will refresh your innermost being." **Before we go on any further......** Why don't you speak to the Holy Spirit? Speak aloud say, "Yes" Lord I am willing to "arise," I do want to drink from the well of living water! Thank You for being my Helper. Amen.

Many a time, when I was almost at the end of life itself and thought that there was no way out, God stepped in time and time again to prevent a terrible tragedy. I would see my beautiful children and experience such love welling up from within that I determined to go on! Yes, you could say I, too, often drank from the well of living water in my wilderness.

However, without a new heart, there can be no lasting hope. The Bible tells us in **Ephesians 2:12** in the Living Bible Translation: *"In those days you were living utterly apart from Christ; you were lost, without God, without hope."* Yet all the time The Divine Eagle could see me. He was working behind the scenes, even though I didn't have any experience personally of His Mercy, His Goodness or His incredible Love. He was waiting for me to respond in faith and allow Him to **find me!**

God has placed in all of us a longing for love that is only satisfied in Him; but without Him, we end up looking for love in all the wrong places. Yes, that is what I did! In my new husband, Skippy, I found a man who idolized me, was kind, loving and attentive in every human way possible, but then neither of us knew any other way! We set up home together, doing what I knew in my heart was wrong, we lived together in an adulterous relationship until we could get married.

Once again The Divine Eagle had work to do. If He had left us in that comfortable nest, we would never have learnt to fly. You see the mother eagle knows that the destiny of her young eaglets is to FLY! Staying in the nest is not the answer so she starts to rip up the nest, taking out the soft feathers, removing all the fluffy down, breaking up the twigs and exposing the sharp thorns; then one by one she gently nudges them to the edge of the overturned nest and pushes one out into the air! The little eaglet, of course, falls like a stone towards the ground, screeching wildly with fear, but just as he is about to hit the ground, the mother eagle swoops down and catches him on her broad wings and carries him safely up into the sky. Then she tilts her wings and flips the young eagle off so he will begin to fall once again. This is repeated time and again until the young eaglet stretches his own wings and begins to fly. The mother eagle is more interested in her young achieving their potential, than in maintaining their comfort zone. **So is God our Divine Eagle!**

Amidst the relative calm of our new home, we experienced the unexpected. We were always "church-goers" and I came face to face with a woman in the church who seemed too good to be true, too happy to be real, and too peaceful for my liking! She took her Sunday school class, which included our twelve year old daughter, to a Christian Conference, and yes, she came back "born again" and quickly told me that I wasn't a Christian! I was not at all pleased.....all the soft feathers of the nest were being removed by the Divine Eagle and I didn't like it! However, we decided to wait to see how our daughter would be. We were amazed; almost immediately her attitudes and behaviour changed for the better! So when the same Conference came back to Aberystwyth the following year, this time I went with her. The Divine Eagle knows how to draw us to Himself.

Perhaps you will know exactly how I felt in the midst of two thousand wildly exuberant, excited Spirit-filled Christians, waving hands and singing in "squeaky" voices. I thought I was in a mad place! However I stayed because I loved my daughter. The Evangelist Don Double spoke, [how we love this man of God now] but I didn't register anything of what he said and there was not even an opportunity to give your heart to Jesus which is truly amazing! However, he did have a prophetic word [as I now understand] saying, "Some people are afraid of the future, or unhappy in their present situations." I was relieved these didn't apply to me. Then he said, "There are some of you here, who, when you think about your past are filled with pain. Only Jesus can take that pain away. Stand up if that is you." I knew it was me, but I was determined not to stand up! Imagine my surprise when I found myself standing.....by now I was too embarrassed to sit down, so I stood while Don prayed, eagerly waiting to just sit again. However, my daughter's Sunday school teacher and her husband noticed that I had stood up and there and then agreed together that they would pray for me until I gave my heart to Jesus. Oh it will be so wonderful to find out one day when we get to Glory who are all these special people who have prayed for us to be saved! Yes the Divine Eagle had a plan and it was all about my surrender to Him, **allowing Him to find me in my wilderness.** *"He scanned me and kept me as the pupil of His eye."*

During the following year, my entire comfort zone, my own nest, was pulled apart by the Divine Eagle Himself. My health began to deteriorate and I even had a head-on car crash with a fractured chest and skull. I also had many severe and dangerous internal haemorrhages and ended up in hospital many times. There were no scans in those days and it was assumed that I had tumours which were possibly cancerous. I eventually ended up in hospital once again at the beginning of December 1979 to have a complete hysterectomy. Thank God for the wings of the Divine Eagle stretched out even there in the hospital; there just happened to be a Pentecostal Minister's wife reading the Bible in the same ward! I had never even heard of a Pentecostal! Seeing her reading the Bible, I thought maybe I should read the Bible too, because although we were "church-goers", we never read the Bible. Now, I suddenly found that I really wanted to read it and remembered that the Gideon's Bible Society often put a Bible for patients use beside the bed in hospitals. The Divine eagle was certainly hovering over my life! I looked for the Bible and found that some child had tied it's ribbon to the knob of the drawer; now I really wanted to read it, so I even asked for a pair of scissors to cut it free. Then sitting cross-legged on the bed, the night before this major operation, for the first time in years I opened the Bible and read **Psalm 23**: *"The Lord is my Shepherd, I shall not want."* I can't say that it spoke to me, but I certainly felt better....the Divine Eagle was fluttering over me!

Several days later after the operation, I was told that apparently the operation had been a success and that there was no cancer. However, instead of my getting better, I got worse and worse - the terrible pain bringing out all of the self-pity, despair, hatred, resentment and bitterness stored up inside me.

At this time, faithfully each day my daughter, would come and read the Bible to me on her way back from school. Many times I did not even hear what she read as I drifted in and out of consciousness. Now I have come to understand that as she read the Word of God, she was releasing the Creative Word of God that always has power and will not fail to do that for which it is sent. How I bless her for doing this every day for almost four weeks. God was certainly the faithful Divine Eagle as he enabled her to do this day after day! At this point my mother and brother came to say goodbye to me, they believed that I was dying.

Christmas came and went and Boxing Day dawned. Another day, an ordinary hospital day - or was it? The Assistant Gynaecologist came to explain that they had discovered a "pocket of blood" and she would snip it with a pair of long surgical tongs, I would bleed a little and then would be better. She did, but there was no "pocket of blood", instead she cut a main artery inside! As everyone panicked around me, my blood was, at first, spurting out like a fountain and then got less and less as the blood pressure lowered. I watched as I lay in my own blood, and saw it spilling over on to the floor. The staff were pumping "blood substitute" into me to keep me alive and as I looked at myself I could see all my bones, vessels and organs through the transparency of my bloodless skin. It is no wonder that people did not recognise the Risen Jesus without His blood! As I looked I knew I was dying and in that moment GRACE Himself came. I found myself speaking out aloud, "Jesus are you really real? If you are, please forgive me, I want to come and be with you forever." If I could explain the absolute miracle that happened in that instant, I would, but I can't! One moment, turmoil and darkness, the next.....Peace, Joy and Love filled my heart with such brilliant light. Oh the Grace of God as the Divine Eagle took me up and bore me on His wings. I heard the Assistant Gynaecologist saying, "You must want to live Mrs Gifford or we cannot save your life." In this amazing peace I replied, "You need Jesus. You serve the wrong god." Did I know anything? No, but in that miraculous moment my spirit-man was made alive and Truth just burst out in overflow!

However, they had to take me back to theatre and it was there that they discovered a large abscess had burst and poison was oozing around my body......without the ruptured artery I would have died anyway! God as my Divine Eagle had everything in control. It was while in theatre that I

9

actually died and went to heaven. I guess that the Divine Eagle swooped down and bore me on His wings so high He stopped off in heaven!

What is heaven like? It was the most beautiful place I had ever been to or seen; I had come "home" where I had always been destined to come to. The Bible says: **Philippians 3:20 Living Bible.** "Our homeland is in heaven." Unlike some people, I did not actually see Jesus, but His Presence was so real; everywhere He was with me. I walked with Him and together we had a oneness of fellowship all the time that I could never have imagined was possible. The colours were so vibrant, the blues more blue, the greens more green, the flowers more exotic and the trees so perfect, as the light exploded through them.....I noticed the long lush grass bent down as I walked on it and yet, as I looked behind me, each individual blade sprang back to life. I gazed at the trees; there were so many leaves, each with its own life - dancing, singing, and moving in harmonious praise to Him. It was "home" wonderful, perfect, and peaceful beyond anything I could ever have dreamed. Then the Spirit of the Father spoke to me, **"I am sending you back, I have a work for you to do."**

I expect you know that God has given everyone of us "free will" and we can use it for good or evil. When we contradict God, that is what He calls the "Sin of Rebellion" and this will separate us from Him.....and I said, "No I want to stay here." This was my first act of rebellion as a Christian and from the wonder of His Majestic Presence, suddenly I was being sucked into an enormous bottomless tunnel of tangible blackness and I couldn't stop myself going down, down, down into an eternity of separation from Him. It was then that my spirit must have cried out. Sometimes, since then, I have seen answers to prayers and yet known that I have not voiced them.....now I understand, God hears the cry of the heart of a born again Believer, just as the Divine Eagle hears the cry of her young! God is Spirit and we can only communicate with Him spirit to Spirit, that is why unbelievers can not have fellowship with God. But now my spirit had been made alive and immediately, in answer to my heart cry, Father God spoke to me in an audible voice. Whatever He had asked me to do I would have done. I have never before or since heard such an amazing voice of command, so powerful, yet so tender, so gentle, personal and loving all at the same time. He said, **"I want you to Breathe Me in when I count: one.... BREATHE...two... BREATHE.... three...BREATHE!"** I did and on the third time, the darkness evaporated never ever to return and light came bursting through....Hallelujah!

The Divine Eagle had swooped down and picked me up yet again and yes, like **Revelation: 12-14** *"The woman was supplied with the two wings of a giant eagle, so that she might fly from the presence of the serpent..."* Yes, I was very weak for several more weeks of recovery in hospital but I was **completely a New Creation in Christ Jesus, I had fallen in love with my Saviour, I was so hungry for the Word of God, I devoured the Bible from cover to cover and worshipped constantly, leading several to know the Lord there in the Hospital.**
John 1:13... *"Who owe their birth neither to bloods nor to the will of the flesh, nor to the will of man, but to God: They are born of God."*
John 3:6.... Jesus said, *"What is born of flesh is flesh, and what is born of the Spirit is spirit."* The Divine Eagle had given me new birth. **Now I was born to FLY! My journey with the Divine Eagle had begun!**

Chapter Two

LEARNING TO FLY

"How I bore you on eagle's wings and brought you to Myself."
Exodus 19:3-4

Webster's Dictionary says: That Eagles are noted for their strength, size, gracefulness, keenness of vision, powers of flight and bright-piercing eyesight......**YET eagles have to learn to fly!**

Eagles represent the Spirit-filled life as opposed to being a carnal or fleshly Christian. You and I are destined to "soar" in the Spirit, and one of the ways that has helped me, is to learn from the eagle. **Proverbs 30:18-19** *"The way of the eagle in the air."* The Bible speaks of this as, *"Too wonderful for me!"*

What sort of a Christian are we then, an **Eagle or a Chicken?** We've all heard of people who say: "Don't be such a chicken", in other words, "Don't be so afraid!" How easy it is to see that that does not reflect a Spirit-filled courageous life, such as an eagle; but rather a Chicken represents our carnal nature. This flesh, which we all have, can never be redeemed.....it has to die! **1 Corinthians 15:31** Paul said, *"I die daily to my flesh."*

Learning to fly means recognising what we are not meant to be. Chickens are fearful, timid birds, seldom flying; they spend their time scratching around in the dust looking for bits of corn among the dirt of the ground. Their focus is constantly downwards, they flap their wings continually, but get nowhere fast.

Hey! Does that sound like you and me at times? Do you remember the video "Chicken Run" and how those battery-bred chickens tried and tried to get out of their captivity and how they made every effort to fly and yet with no avail? It is not hard to see how this represents our flesh life; how we too often use our own effort, become frustrated and the Spirit is quenched - and we wonder why we have all the difficulties!

Jesus said: **John 6:63** *"The flesh conveys no benefit whatever."*

Paul said: **Romans 7:18** *"I know nothing good dwells within me that is in my flesh."*

And again in **Romans 8:7** *"The flesh is hostile to God."*

Or in **Romans 13:14** *"Make no provision for the flesh."*

Chickens live a very limited and contained life centred on being "fattened" artificially for us to eat, or bred to produce as many eggs as possible to make money for their owners! Could it be that we might only live, in a measure, like that: to look good, feel good and do good; satisfied in having our salvation ticket, but not fulfiling our God-given destiny to **FLY in the Spirit?** Jesus was very harsh towards this sort of religiosity. He called it "Hypocrisy."

Matthew 7:5 Jesus said, *"First get the beam of timber out of your own eye."*

Matthew 23: 26 *"First clean the inside of the cup."* Most of us, if we are honest, know that there is a bit of a chicken inside us that has to go. So I urge you to acknowledge the chicken that is hidden inside you and believe, as you ask the Holy Spirit to remove it, He will do just that and you will be ready to: **Learn to Fly!**

It would be so good to pray together now....

Father, I come to You in The Name of Jesus and in the Power of the Holy Spirit; I admit that I often get agitated and strive and act more like a "chicken" than an "eagle", please forgive me for all my fearfulness. Holy Spirit please help me not to react in a fleshly way, but to respond to You and allow You to take control of every situation. Teach me Lord I pray, I so want to learn to fly in The Spirit more and more. Amen.

Take time with The Holy Spirit and listen to His gentle whisper, be real and honest and willing to be obedient to whatever He says to you.......You will be amazed and thrilled how close He draws you to Himself!

Eagles represent **'Life in the Spirit'** and we need to bridge the gap from a fearful, carnal life of a Chicken, to one that is full of new horizons filled with joy, peace, purpose and excitement in the Holy Spirit! Is it possible? **YES!** Let us look at Jesus; He is our perfect example always - Jesus was born of the Spirit. **Luke 1:35** *"He shall be called The Son of God."* We too are born again by the power of the Holy Spirit. The Spirit makes Jesus real to us; convicting us of our need and desire for the Saviour. Take notice that Jesus did no works of power, nor did He begin His ministry UNTIL AFTER He had been empowered by the Holy Spirit at His Baptism. This was when God, The Father, publicly approved and affirmed Jesus as His own Beloved Son and The Holy Spirit descended upon Him in bodily form, like a dove.
Mark 1:10 *"Like a dove coming down to enter into Him."*
John 1:32 *"As a dove out of heaven, and it dwelt on Him never to depart."* Only then are we told in **Matthew 4:1** *"Jesus full of and controlled by The Holy Spirit was led into the wilderness to be tempted by the devil."*
Luke 4:14 *"Then Jesus went back full of, and under the power of, the Holy Spirit."*

If we look at the young eagles we can learn more about how to fly in the Spirit, even in wilderness situations! Once a mother has literally pushed the young eaglets out of the nest, [and **remember not one of them will ever leave willingly**] and when the young eagle has eventually learnt to use its own wings to be air borne THEN, and only then, is he ready to **learn to fly** according to the various conditions, and build up his own strength and handle himself as an eagle!

His strength is known to be in his **DIET** and he will never eat any dead animal, even when hungry. He has even been known to ignore a dead salmon in a river, willing to wait until he finds one alive. The eagle needs also to learn how to handle the different **WINDS**; how to spread his wings so that the thermals provide the power he needs to soar above and go higher. This is important as smaller birds try to irritate and pester the eagle from behind, but what he does is that he just soars to another level using the winds to get away from them! Remember in **Song of Songs 3:15** *"Take from us the little foxes that spoil the vineyards, for our vineyards are in blossom."* It is always the little things that creep up seemingly from behind in some unexpected way! How wonderful if we too, like the eagle, could just soar to another level in the Holy Spirit every time things irritate or frustrate us! I believe it is possible! We need to learn to fly!

As we progress together, make this your heart felt prayer........ Holy Spirit teach me to soar above the little things that try to hinder me, I want to learn to fly and be like the eagle. Amen.

The eagle has to learn how to **SWOOP DOWN** to capture his prey, to time the descent and judge the distance to great precision. This is an important part of the eagle learning to fly. Where does the young eagle learn this? He has been born to fly: this is his destiny. It is in his DNA to be king of all the birds, fearless and majestic.

But still the eagle has to learn and it is **IN THE WILDERNESS** that he **LEARNS TO FLY.** Probably the greatest learning curve for me happened during the time before my husband Skippy became a Christian. I had to learn how to depend entirely on the Holy Spirit, lean on His Word and establish my own relationship with God in prayer. Was it easy? No, but I wouldn't have missed that time for anything and I believe that it was essential in my growth as a Spirit-filled Christian. Maybe you are in a similar situation.....It **would be good if we prayed together:**

Lord Jesus, I really feel alone, I seem to be experiencing a wilderness time in my life, but I am asking You now to help me trust You in every situation so that I can learn to fly in The Spirit and not waste this learning opportunity. Thank You Lord. Amen.

What happens to the young eagle is that suddenly he seems to be all alone; no Mama or Papa to provide for him. They are not there to direct him or even protect him. He has all the potential and his wings are able to carry him even as high as 80,000 feet. At his peak he will be able to swoop down at 200 miles per hour. Now comes the hard part! He has to learn to grow, to develop, to deal with the adverse conditions and he has to **learn to fly!** When a storm comes the eagle does not screech and hide as the chicken does, [he senses a storm before he actually sees it] but he "locks" his wings in an "up-ward tilt." God has created the eagle with a very special device; on either side of his shoulders, where the wings meet the main body, there is a small muscle that the eagle can choose to "lock" or "set" so that his wings are ready for **take off!** This action of the eagle reflects how we too can make our choices to act in the flesh or access everything we need from our spirit-man.

A wonderful story illustrates this so well....I am told it is true and took place once again in Australia! A chicken farmer went out with his young son one day hiking into the mountains and there they came across an eagle's nest with no sign of the eagles. However, inside they saw three eggs, which the farmer knew would not hatch if they were left alone. So not wanting to remove all of the eggs, they carefully took just one of them home and found a nice broody chicken who was only too happy to sit on the egg!!!

Eventually the day came when the young eagle hatched and the chicken was delighted with her new "chick" and there after she began to teach it all she knew about scratching on the ground for food and flapping her wings! The chicken didn't realize that her young chick was different, until one day, a storm was heading towards the chicken farm. She followed all the other chickens and ran fearfully for the shelter of the sheds, but to her surprise the young eagle was happy to stay outside and seemed to enjoy the windy conditions! The young eagle had a different DNA, and even though he believed he was a chicken, when the conditions changed.....he reacted as an eagle!

Now the farmer saw what was happening, and in good faith he decided that the young eagle needed protecting, so he clipped his wings to keep him safe in the chicken enclosure. When I heard this, it really reminded me that often people can clip our spiritual wings thinking that they are protecting us...Saying things like, "be careful about using the spiritual gifts you are not yet mature enough" or "you will soon find the honeymoon period is over and you won't be so radical!" Yes, many of us were wounded and found our spiritual wings were clipped in our early days as a Christian. Maybe even now you can relate to what I am saying? Very recently, I was doing a "Prophetic Encounter Day Conference" and so many people who were there had had bad experiences several years ago. They needed healing from those hurtful situations before they could move forward and use the gifts that they had in the Holy Spirit and begin again to fly in The Spirit.

Amazingly ....as we look at the eagle we learn that the feathers begin to grow again very quickly and the young eagle, in the story, was soon able to stretch its wings. Then one day a big storm arrived and the young eagle flew up on to his favourite place, the highest post, while all the other chickens ran for cover as usual! Suddenly as he perched up on the post he heard a sound he'd never heard before.....A fully grown eagle "screeched" in the stormy clouds high above him...he was so startled that he spread his wings and at once the wind currents swept him up, up and up high into the sky and he was flying! He was free to be who he was always meant to be, free from the fences and barriers that the chickens were content to live in. He was free! We too must allow the wind of the Spirit to lift us up and free us from all the constrictions so that we can be free to fly.

For this to happen we may need to forgive and be healed from all the things that could have clipped our spiritual wings.....

Let us pray:

Father, I now realize how wounded I am and I choose to forgive those, who for whatever reason, were used to clip my spiritual wings. I want to move on and learn to fly in all the wonderful things of the Spirit. Please will You teach me Holy Spirit once again how to use my spiritual wings? Thank You Lord. Amen.

In the wilderness the eagle chooses what he eats, resisting the possible poison of a dead carcass; he chooses to set his wings so he can soar above the storm and he learns how to perfect the downward dive so that he is able to catch and kill his prey and doesn't miss it. Above all he needs to **read the wilderness** and make it work for his good.....**Because the eagle is born to fly! As a Spirit-filled Christian we are born to fly too!**

So now let us allow the Holy Spirit to give us revelation and insight as to what happened to Jesus in the wilderness. Jesus is always our perfect example, He was led by the Spirit into the desert where He shows us how we too can overcome and how we can deal with difficulties that the devil would throw our way. To fly as an eagle, we have to come through our own wilderness experiences, no one can do this for us. We have to learn for ourselves how to grow and **come out in the power of the Spirit as Jesus did.**
Luke 4:14 *"Jesus came out in the Power of the Spirit"*

In my experience I have known so many wonderful people with a very real anointing from God and yet they never seem to reach their potential. I asked the Holy Spirit to show me what had happened and I saw, in the Spirit, that they were often led by the Spirit into the wilderness but because of pressures, situations and people, they would retreat out of the wilderness when the going got really tough. I sensed the sadness of the Holy Spirit who so wanted to bring them out in the power of the Spirit to fulfil their destiny; but He couldn't, because of the choices they had made.

Firstly I believe that Jesus has shown us that there can be no short cut. We have to **learn to "set" our spiritual wings** in an upward tilt, yes we are to make Godly choices or we too will be destroyed at the first hint of a storm. This is our "power of choice" it is our free will that we need to exercise; to decide once and for all, as Jesus Himself did in the garden: **Matthew 26: 39** *"Not My will but Yours be done."* There can be no going backwards. The old song said it so well, "I have decided to follow Jesus, no turning back, no turning back. Though none go with me yet will I follow, no turning back, no turning back!" To **learn to fly** we need to set our will, to "lock" our spiritual wings. The devil will keep testing us time and time again until he knows it's useless because we have **chosen** and **purposed** in our hearts that we will not go back, but we will go on **whatever it takes**. Esther had to come to this final decision.

Esther 4:16: *"If I perish, I perish, but I WILL go into the king."* Every one of us has to come to that decision for ourselves if we are to live the Spirit-filled life as an eagle and come out of our wilderness in the power of the Spirit.

Secondly, Jesus was challenged at the point of His **greatest need which was His hunger**. That was His place of vulnerability and need after He had fasted for 40 days and He was hungry! The devil will always be allowed to test us on the priority of our desires because the devil always wants us to be selfish and self-centred and to use the power of God to benefit ourselves.

Luke 4:3-4: *"If you are the Son of God, turn this stone into a loaf of bread." Jesus answered: "It is written, Man shall not live by bread alone, but by every word proceeding out of the mouth of God."* Jesus was quoting from **Deut 8:3:** You are what you eat! Esau lost his birthright and his inheritance all because he allowed his immediate hunger to be more important than his future in God. He forfeited everything because he just wanted to satisfy his own desires. You will find that the enemy will always stir up our fleshly desires so that we think they are more important and of a greater priority than our destiny.

Beware of what we eat .....there are several ways we can feed on the wrong things:

1. The **Eye Gate:** Is an open door to the enemy if we do not

watch what we watch on TV, guard what we see on the Internet and be very careful what we read; especially in pornographic or lewd magazines or books or even newspapers. This can produce a spiritual weakness which will make it hard to resist the devil, and you will never come out of the wilderness in the Power of the Spirit. Sometimes something will happen that is beyond our control, if I share an example I am sure that you will understand. I was a guest in someone's house and went to use their computer, as I opened it to my horror some really bad images came up on the screen. My eye gate had seen what was not good and I found it very hard to wipe the images from my mind. So I immediately contacted my husband [brought it into the light] and together we prayed, and later I took "bread and wine" to re-consecrate myself under the blood and re-establish "covenant" with the Lord. This is not the only way, but it works for me, and we need to keep our eye gate pure whatever happens!

2. The **Ear Gate:** Is another entrance for negative feeding on dead things that will poison your spirit such as listening to gossip, criticism or negative and worldly talk. Lustful or evil music is also very dangerous too and gives ground to the devil to pull you backwards and will keep you in the wilderness.

3. The **Mouth Gate: Proverbs 18:21** *"The power of death and life is in the power of the tongue, and those who indulge in it shall eat the fruit of it for death or life."* Check yourself, **check what you are eating,** you will discover this by what comes out of your mouth! Ask the Holy Spirit to show you, He is The Helper. A little while ago I was talking to the Holy Spirit about feeling tired and I was so surprised that he immediately reminded me how I was always saying how tired I was!! Needless to say I decided to change what I was saying straightaway! Often we speak negative things without

realizing and it gives ground to the enemy. STOP NOW! Jesus confronted every temptation in the wilderness by: "It is written." He knew the power of the Word of God and used it as a two-edged sword. David knew how important his mouth was and we need to realize this too.

Psalm 39:1 David said, *"I will take heed and guard my ways, that I may not sin with my tongue; I will muzzle my mouth as with a bridle.."*

Psalm19:14 *"Let the words of my mouth and the meditation of my heart be acceptable in Your sight O Lord."*

Hebrews 4:12: *"The Word that God speaks is alive and full of power, sharper than any two-edged sword, exposing and sifting and analyzing and judging the very thoughts and purposes of the heart."* Wow, we need that to grow and learn to fly....**Use these scriptures to personally pray:** Holy Spirit will You enable me to put a muzzle on my mouth, so that everything I speak will be acceptable in Your sight O Lord. Amen.

There is another temptation, that Jesus encountered, that was: **TO BY-PASS THE CROSS.......**

Luke 4:5: Satan tempted Jesus, *"I will give you all this power and authority of all the kingdoms of the world, if you will just worship me."* This is **non-negotiable.** **NEVER** have a conversation with the devil even when he might appear to offer you what you want! Jesus said, *"Get thee behind Me satan."* You do the same!

At the cross Jesus defeated ALL the powers of darkness, Jesus cried out in victory "**It is Finished.**" It was then on the Cross that Jesus won the supreme victory, He paid the price with His Blood to give us Salvation and by His stripes we are healed. He took our punishment, our rejection, our pains, grief's and sorrows and when we BELIEVE in Jesus Christ THEN we have the free gift of ETERNAL LIFE...Hallelujah! **No wonder he shouted...It is finished! Everything was accomplished and God RAISED HIM**

UP from the dead!
Hebrews 9:26 *"It was the perfect sacrifice once for all."*
Colossians 2:15: *"God disarmed the principalities and powers that were ranged against us and made a public bold display of them in triumphing over them in Him and in the cross."* Remember **the devil is a liar!** You have everything when you have Christ, you are complete in Him, and the devil only wants to deceive us into thinking that if we just worship him we will have what we want......**NO!** We are to worship the One True Living God, Who alone is Worthy.

For an eagle there can be no short cut to getting his prey, it is his way of life; he has to learn to swoop, to judge and time his amazing descent and not be lured into the trap of going for a dead animal that could kill him. **Our way of life depends on what Jesus has done for us on the cross.**

In fact, I believe we ALL need to come **THROUGH the cross.** I find there are many unstable Christians that have allowed themselves to become ensnared because they only know ABOUT the cross; they believe that Jesus died for them and washed their sins away, even realizing that Christ is risen from the dead **YET** have not encountered, personally, the God of the cross. Paul said:
Galatians 2:20: NIV *"I have been crucified with Christ, it is no longer I who live, but Christ that lives within me, and the life that I now live, I live by the faith of the Son of God Who loved me and gave His life for me."* The Amplified Bible goes further: *"I have shared His crucifixion."*

Here I would like to share my personal testimony that happened only weeks after my life-changing encounter with the Lord. As I devoured and read the Word of God, I began to feel dirty on the inside. Words such as "adultery" would stand out to me; I did not have any understanding of what conviction of sin involved; I just knew I loved Jesus with all my heart and this feeling of uncleanness was not nice! However, it increased until one day I began to sob uncontrollably and cry out to God, "How can I be clean? Lord I love you, but I want to be clean so you can fill more of me". Almost at once I began to see a video-film of the Crucifixion in my spirit-man. I watched as Jesus carried His cross, I saw His skin ripped off, I saw where the splinters of wood were sticking into the raw flesh. I knew He was going to be crucified and I began to cry out, "It's not fair, He's done nothing wrong" but no-one seemed to take any notice, they continued to nail Him to the cross; each hammer blow resounding in my innermost being. I watched as people pulled out parts of His beard, I saw them bash the large clumps of six inch thorns on the top of His head. It was hideous, as the blood spurted out, running down His face. I saw the way His shoulder joints were dislocated as the weight of His body pulled and stretched His arms away from the nail-pierced hands. I had never seen anything so horrific and I actually shouted again, this time much louder...."Don't do it to Him, He is innocent." Then as I watched, I saw the Centurion, with his sword, go towards Jesus; I knew what he was going to do.....I screamed again and again, "NO, NO don't do it!" I actually felt the terrible piercing pain as the sword shot through His side, the blood coming out in one river and water coming out in another river. **THEN.......The Centurion turned, it wasn't him....... it was ME!** In that instant, the Spirit of the Father spoke, not in condemnation, but in truth, "That is what your adultery did to My Son." The horror of what my sin had done throbbed in every part of me. I was a murderer; I had killed the Son of God:

Acts 2:23: Paul said, *"You crucified Him."*

Since then I have come to know that this was prophesied in:

Zechariah 12:10: *"They shall look upon Him whom they have pierced, and they shall mourn for Him."*

John 19:37: *"They shall look on Him whom they have pierced."*

Revelation 1: 7: *"Every eye will see Him, even those who pierced Him."*

I believe that there is only one cry anyone could make when you see what your sins have really done and that is **"HAVE MERCY!"** In that moment I knew I deserved everlasting hell, but the Bible says: **"mercy triumphs over justice at the Cross!"** The Merciful One, in that instant, overflowed me with His precious blood, it just surged over me and inside me and **I became snow white clean!** The voice of Jesus whispered and I saw Him move His head to look at me and say, **"I forgive you." Oh the joy of sins forgiven....** I knew I was clean!

What response can anyone have in the face of such utter mercy? All I can say is that an over-whelming love and gratitude rose up from deep within me and I said over and over again: "Oh Thank You, thank you, thank you and I seemed to run out of English words and I began to speak in languages I had never heard before. It was as if it was a love-language, spirit to Spirit, expressing my thanks better than I could manage. It was bubbling up from deep within my heart! I began to realize that I could stop and start as I chose, but when I was quiet, then I would hear the Spirit speaking to me: "I love you, you are precious, you are My Child, I have Chosen you, I have called you by name." Such was the ecstasy that my spirit began to overflow again and again. Time stood still and I had no idea what had happened to me, except it was SO wonderful and hearing His voice so clearly was amazing! Now, of course, I have come to understand that this was what Jesus had spoken of to the Disciples:

Luke 24:49: *"Wait in the city until you are clothed with power from on high."*
Mark 16:17 *"You will speak in new languages."*
Acts 1:5: *"You shall be baptised with the Holy Spirit.*

Acts 1:8: *"You shall receive power, ability, efficiency and might when the Holy Spirit has come upon you."* But then I did not have any understanding, just the marvellous experience of the cross and resurrection. **I had come to know that I had been crucified with Christ and I would never be the same again!**

Coming out of your wilderness in the power of the Spirit will always involve the Cross and His empowering. It will not be like my experience, God has one especially for you. However, similar principles always apply......**Power comes from the Resurrection!**

Just recently I was with a lovely man of God and he began to tell me his story of how he was asked, as an unbeliever, to make a big wooden cross as part of the Easter celebrations. As he was nailing it together, suddenly he saw himself hitting the nails into the hands and feet of Jesus and blood began spurting out onto his hands as he held the hammer. There and then, amid many tears, he bowed to Jesus and was completely born again. What a WONDERFUL Saviour we have!

If you are not sure that you have ever come through the cross..... **PRAY** and I promise that you will never be the same!

O Precious Jesus, thank You for dying for me on the cross, I am not sure that I have truly had an experience of the cross. Lord, reveal to me by the power of the Holy Spirit just what my sin did to You so that I will know that I have been crucified with You. Thank You Lord. Amen.

We are led by the Spirit into the wilderness, not to stay there, but to come out in the power of the Spirit to exercise our "spiritual wings" and rise above all temptations and ride the wind thermals of the Spirit; feeding on the Bread of Life, and taught by the Spirit of God. He is the very best teacher! **John 14:26:** *"He will teach you all things, the Holy Spirit Whom the Father will send in My Name."* Learning to fly is part of our DNA too. **Eagles must learn to fly, so must you to fulfil your destiny!**

Chapter Three

SOARING TO VICTORY

"As Eagles mount up to the sun"
Isaiah 40:31

Job 39: 27: *"Does the Eagle mount up at your command and make his nest on a high inaccessible place? On the cliff he dwells and remains securely, upon the point of the rock and the stronghold."*

You are an eagle in your spirit-man not a grasshopper.

Numbers 13: 33: *"We were in our own eyes as grasshoppers and so we were in their sight."* No, they weren't, but that was what they believed and it cost them forty years delay in entering the Promised Land. It is crucial how you see yourself if you are going to **soar to victory**..... So the first and most important vision has to be that you know who you are in Christ and what you have in Him. To be spiritually victorious is not possible on enthusiasm alone.

Let me share one good example when enthusiasm was not enough: As a Church one year we had a word for "Outreach" into the community, to take part in the town Carnival with bright yellow helium balloons painted with "Jesus Loves you". It was really very successful and so the next year we were enthusiastic to do it again. However, this time it was just our own fleshly decision and it bore no fruit at all! To be successful and soar in victory as the eagle we need to know that the Spirit initiates everything and this will bring real lasting fruitfulness. The eagle has to use his power and then he has to utilize it to **soar above** every situation and circumstance.

When we are filled with the Spirit we need to believe what the Word says:

Ephesians 1:19-20: *"Know and understand what is the immeasurable and unlimited and surpassing greatness of His power in and for you who believe, as demonstrated in the working of His mighty strength which He exerted in Christ when He raised Him from the dead and seated Him at the right hand in the heavenly places...**Far above all!**"* That surpassed everything and anything...and God did it! If He could raise Christ from the dead, then He can do all things IN and FOR us who believe.

1 John 4: 4: *"You are of God and have already defeated and overcome, because, He that is in you is greater than he who is in the world."* Jesus told His Disciples that they would have tribulation, BUT....

John 16:33: Jesus said, *"I have overcome and conquered it for you."*

If we take a look at how the eagle rises out of turbulence we will learn valuable lessons: They use the hot air thermals that rush upwards and lift them towards the heavens; these same winds would dash them to pieces and destroy them if they stayed on the ground. We desperately need to find the hot air currents of Grace, Praise and Love that will not let us go and then fully co-operate with the Spirit even when we feel everything is out of control.

2 Corinthians 12:9 Paul said, *"My grace is enough for you...My strength and power are made perfect and show themselves most effective in your weakness."*

Colossians 3: 1-2 *"If then you have been raised with Christ to a brand new life, thus sharing His resurrection from the dead, aim at and seek the rich eternal treasures that are above, where Christ is seated at the right hand of God. **Set your minds and keep them set on what is above,** the higher things, not on the things that are on the earth."*

1. To live in the supernatural realm requires that the Word works for you.

You need to be speaking the Word of God and become a "doer" of the Word.

Isaiah 55: 11: *"So shall My word be that goes forth from My mouth; it shall not return to Me void, but it shall accomplish that for which I please and purpose, and it shall prosper in the thing for which I sent it."* The Spirit of God prophesied:

Isaiah 51: 16: *"I have put My words in your mouth and have covered you with the shadow of My hand."* Many years ago I came to realize and believe that there was power in God's Word.

2 Timothy 3: 16: *"Every scripture is God-breathed, given by His inspiration and profitable....so that the man [and woman] of God may be complete and proficient, well fitted and thoroughly equipped for every good work."* I began to learn how to use these Spiritual thermals to take me above the situations. God began to "highlight" certain words as I needed them in various circumstances. I decided to **agree with His Word**, set my spiritual wings so to speak, and start **confessing that particular Word with thanksgiving** over and over again. We are told that Abraham did this:

Romans 4: 17-18: *"He spoke of those non-existent things, that God had foretold and prophesied, as if they already existed....he grew strong and was empowered by faith as he gave praise and glory to God."*

Let me give you an example. Our family at that time was full of strife and division, with no knowledge of how to work together in harmony and peace and this was causing a lot of heartache. I sought for the Spirit to help us, [and remember He is the Counsellor and Helper] and one day, almost when I had forgotten how I had cried to Him for help, a Word jumped out at me from the portion of scripture I was reading in the Good News Bible at the time.....

30

Isaiah 60: 22: *"Even the smallest and humblest family will become as great as a powerful nation. When the right time comes I will make it happen quickly, I am the Lord."* God had breathed on to this particular portion of Scripture and to me it became a **Rhema Word.** It became a "quickened NOW word" as the Holy Spirit breathed life on to it. Faith flowed into my heart and I began to confess the word with thanksgiving, literally hundreds of times week after week, whenever the Spirit reminded me. Oh the wonder, His Word works! God brought it to pass. Our testimony is that we are now a family united and all our children and our children's children love and serve the Lord. That is a miracle! I say this to stimulate your faith, so that you can begin to **"soar"** above and see the Holy Spirit bring victories to every situation and to change the seemingly unchangeable circumstances. Ride the wind thermals of His Word and you'll never be the same again. Eagles work with the winds; we need to work with the Spirit and see what He will do.....then be sure you give Him all the Glory.

2. To live in the supernatural realm requires that you are not passive.

The eagle makes his nest on the high cliff up on the solid rock. It is meant to last, weighing 2-3 tons and can be as much as 20 feet wide, 8 feet high and 10 feet deep. There it is built on solid rock underneath, behind and around it and is a very safe place against all predators; it is known as a stronghold or a fortress. The male and female eagle choose it together, they work together to build it and together they maintain it. They are very active in moving together towards their future. We need to build our nest on the high cliff on the solid rock of His Word that will never pass away.

Psalm 1: 1: *"Blessed is the man who walks not in the counsel of the ungodly nor stands submissive and **inactive** in the path where sinners walk."* One of the greatest dangers for us Christians is to be passive to the enemy.

31

LET US LOOK AT THE EAGLE:

Without question, he is by far the most bold, fearless and powerfully active of all birds. No wonder he is known as the king of all birds. Yet, amazingly, these very characteristics seem to completely change when he finds himself **in captivity**. In fact, the whole personality of the eagle is transformed because God never created him to be controlled, manipulated or intimidated and so it is with us. Our real born again personality is to soar above in Christ, but it can also change dramatically when we allow ourselves, or find ourselves, in any sort of captivity. It could be in bondage to: SIN, SICKNESS, DECEPTION, CURSES, FEARS and the PAST or even to PEOPLE we may want to please. Fear of man brings its own snare and will cause us to become **passive to the enemy** and lose our spiritual authority so that we become unable to soar to victory, finding ourselves in one sort of captivity or another. Eagles in captivity are even content to eat dead meat that often poisons them; they cease to clean themselves, and lose all aggressive behaviour to the point that they have been known to allow a small rat to eat away at their legs little by little while they are asleep.

Could this be a picture of us in our own prisons such as: depression, self-pity or fears that may have ensnared us and made us passive to the enemy? If it is, the devil will take full advantage of us and begin to **eat away at our faith**, sowing seeds of doubt and unbelief, without us even being aware of his cunning plan. We may even find ourselves accepting his foul lies as he infiltrates with the most negative of thoughts which we begin to believe. These are some of the negative things the devil has thrown my way: "You are too old." "You are not good enough." What if people knew what you were really like?" "Your past is worse than anyone else's." "What has happened is your fault, so God won't help you now."........**NO! The devil is a liar!** He works with what we

32

believe, and when we accept his lies, we are becoming passive and he will, bit by bit, erode our faith about 'who God is' and 'who we are in Christ.' The enemy is after our confidence in God, so no wonder the Bible tells us in:

Hebrews 10: 35: *"Do not, therefore, fling away your fearless confidence."* My husband has so often encouraged me with this Scripture when I have been on the point of feeling sorry for myself, anxious or worried. Yes it happens to all of us! But immediately we need to resist all passivity and not throw away our confidence. Recognise the ploy of the enemy!

The eagle even though he is in captivity has not lost his abilities .....He just thinks he has! What we think really does matter.

Proverbs 23:7: *"As a man thinks in his heart, so is he."* **Could this happen to us?**

Perhaps we are not reading the Word as we used to, not cleansing ourselves with the Word as it says:

Ephesians 5: 26: *"We are washed by the water of the Word."*

Becoming passive to the tactics of the enemy often results in abandoning sweet fellowship with the Body of Christ; we tend to ignore the so-called 'little sins' and the hidden attitudes that no one sees. There is a tendency in every one of us to start making excuses for being passive, but before we know it we are well and truly backslidden and in a measure of captivity to the enemy. You will know this is true when you can remember a time when you were more passionate about Jesus than you are now.....Oh help us Lord!

1 John 1: 7: *"If we really do live and walk in the Light as He is in the Light, we have fellowship with one another and the blood of Christ cleanses us from all sin and guilt."*

These hidden things can creep in and fester inside us, because the blood of Jesus Christ is only able to cleanse what we are prepared to confess. Let us be sure we are clean and stay clean before a Holy God and **soar above in victory!**

3. To live in the supernatural realm requires us to be free of all spiritual poison.

The eagle has been created to feed on 'live meat' and yet in captivity he is content to feed on dead meat which often poisons him, by feeding on the 'leftovers' and carcasses of putrefied animals just to satisfy his hunger. This speaks to me so much that it is possible that, we too, can feed off the handouts from other people, instead of getting the 'Fresh Bread' of the Word of God by the Spirit of God direct to our hearts. Maybe we do not feel confident to search the Word for ourselves, or perhaps we just feed on the Sunday Sermon thinking mistakenly that that is sufficient.... and so it becomes our only food for the week! Other types of handouts can be; feeding solely on 'Christian Television' or Christian books. Good as they may be, it can be a very unbalanced diet and very unhealthy and it should never be a substitute for going to church. The only time the eagle feeds on regurgitated food is when he is still in the nest and has not yet learnt to get his own food. The Bible says:

Hebrews 5: 12-14: *"Everyone who continues to feed on milk is obviously inexperienced and unskilled in the doctrine of righteousness, a mere infant!"*

In the wild, free life, God has created the eagle with a very special pattern of behaviour to get rid of all accidental poisoning from his body. Immediately the eagle recognises the poisonous symptoms in his body, he flies to the highest exposed rock where, he literally **"spread eagles"** himself [yes, that is where we get the word] and he stays there until the heat of the burning rays of the sun draw out all the poison and he is restored! Hallelujah.......what a picture of the **Redeeming, Restoring Presence of the Son of Righteousness, Who rises with healing in His wings (Malachi 4: 2).** We certainly need to emulate the eagles behaviour, learning to quickly humble ourselves before the burning, searching eyes of the Son of God Himself, and allow the Holy Spirit to draw out all the poison of accumulated bitterness, unforgiveness, anger, frustration, rejection, resentment, self-pity or just what's stuck to us from being in the world.....**and receive the healing provided at the CROSS.**

I remember several years ago at a Conference where I was ministering, there was a young woman who got right with God. She had many different things that had "stuck to her" and as she willingly forgave and responded to the Holy Spirit. I could see her countenance was glowing and I gently asked her if she would like to share what was happening to her. I shall never forget her reply, she laughed and said how the Holy Spirit had taken all the velcrose off so nothing could stick to her in the future!! The truth is if our attitudes are righteous and we are close to the Lord and overflowing in His holy anointing oil....then nothing will stick to us! **But** to avoid quality time in His Presence, for whatever reason, leaves us in danger of perpetual passivity and enemy occupation instead of being a holy temple for the Spirit of God.

1 Corinthians 6: 19: *"Do you not know that your body is the temple, the very sanctuary of the Holy Spirit Who lives in you Whom you have received as a Gift from God? You are not your own, you were purchased, bought with a price and made His own."*

4. To live in the supernatural realm requires us to keep our vision.

Perhaps, one of the saddest things about an eagle in captivity is that, although he still has his remarkable eye sight, he loses his vision. The cage or enclosure limits his immediate perspective and he is no longer able to see beyond the barriers of his captivity and he cannot use what God has created in him.

You might wonder how this could apply to our spiritual ability to **soar above**. How can we learn from the eagle? Perhaps you have had a 'word,' 'a dream,' a prophetic word or perhaps a vision from the Holy Spirit? Then because it has never come to pass, been delayed or just seems so impossible....you have allowed it to be stolen by the enemy. Maybe it has not quite gone but it has almost been snuffed out? For myself, I almost let go of the vision of being a preacher so many times because it seemed so impossible, in those early days women just were not accepted! But then in some way the Holy Spirit would encourage me and the vision was re-ignited by some person of God or a Word would become personal in the Bible or many times it would be my husband. Praise God the Holy Spirit never let it die completely! Perhaps, like me, you have something that you have not quite let go of....

Let us agree together....Father, I ask that You would once again breathe on this seed in this precious Child by Your Holy Spirit, let life come flooding back and encourage them to know it will come to pass in Jesus' Name. Amen.

The Bible says:

Proverbs 29: 18: *"Where there is no vision the people perish."*

I meet so many lovely Christians who have let the devil steal these promises and I know that it makes the Holy Spirit so sad because we all need to have God's purpose and desires for our lives. Paul never lost his vision, even in prison.

Philippians 3: 14: *"Forgetting what lies behind and straining forward to what lies ahead, I press on toward the goal of the high calling in Christ Jesus."* In fact the amazing blind woman, Helen Keller said: "There is only one thing that is worse than being blind, is having sight but no vision." Yes as we have prayed let the Holy Spirit reignite your dream, your vision or your secret desire that has been dulled, stolen or just buried under the pressures of life. He is the Life-Giving Spirit who would love to breathe into your vision once again. Dare to be an eagle and let the Spirit take you to the rock that is higher than you!

Isaiah 61: 2-4: *"For You have been a shelter and a refuge for me, a strong tower against the adversary… I trust in the shelter of Your wings."* He is Your Divine Eagle and he will enable you to **soar to victory**.

Earlier in my life, God had spoken to me in a most unusual way: he used my husband, who was unsaved at the time, to waken me in the middle of the night to tell me that God had a message for me! Don't put God in a box; if He could use a donkey to speak to Balaam, He can use anyone! That message profoundly impacted my life as it confirmed all that the Spirit of God had already shared with me. [Remember it should always confirm to you what God has already been saying personally, and it will never contradict the Word of God]. Basically the message said: "I am calling you to go into the world and preach the Gospel, be bold and inspire people to live like Jesus." However, as I have said, for years this seemed completely impossible as women were only allowed to serve on the Mission field. The result was that I quenched this vision deep inside me and often became frustrated as there seemed no way this could come to pass….so little by little I almost allowed the adversary to steal my calling and my destiny.

So you see there was a time, when I too, needed to go to the rock that was higher than I; where I allowed the Son of Righteousness and His Presence to draw out all the poisonous unbelief that had seeped in and to ask The Holy Spirit to revitalize the vision.

Now, by His amazing grace, I am actually living in my vision and seeing it unfold before my eyes. Soaring to victory is my experience, even as I travel to different countries around the world. I have to 'smile'; some even call me "the eagle woman!"

Chapter Four

SWOOP TO VICTORY

"Like the eagle that swoops down on the prey."
Job 9: 26

Deuteronomy 28: 48: *"As swift as the eagle flies."*
Habakkuk 1: 8: *"Fly like an eagle that hastens to devour."*

It is established that the eagle goes higher in adversity than at any other time. In other words, the storm lifts the eagle to a higher potential then he would otherwise experience without the storm! The eagle is never afraid of any storm; he has learnt to '**embrace**' the storm. So we too, as Spirit-filled Christians, need to learn not just to use the hot air currents of the wind thermals to soar above, but to see the potential that every storm has; to actually lift us up higher and closer into the Manifest Presence of God Himself. Hidden in the storm is the **potential** for us to grow in character to be like Christ and to soar to new levels. This must be good news for every Believer as this is God's purpose for each of us:

Romans 8: 29: *"Those He foreknew, He also destined from the beginning, to be moulded into the image of His Son."* That is our awesome potential in Christ. **How is this possible?**

Habakkuk 3: 16-19: *"Though the fig tree does not blossom and there is no fruit on the vines, though the product of the olive fails and the field yields no food, though the flock is cut off from the fold and there are no cattle in the stalls.... Yet will I rejoice in the Lord; I will exult in the victorious God of my salvation. The Lord God is my Strength, my personal bravery, and my invincible army; He makes my feet like hinds' feet and will make me to walk [not stand still in terror, but to walk] and make spiritual progress upon my high places of trouble, suffering or responsibility."*

That has to be one of my favourite Scriptures; it has helped me so many times. Perhaps, like me, you too have had those moments of difficulty:

"Though the unexpected happens..... Though something should have happened, but didn't..... Though everything appears to crash all around you...... Though you've done your best but at the last moment someone lets you down..... Though you can see no way forward......Though there is no provision at all......**YET, God turned up, maybe at the last moment, but He didn't fail you as you embraced the storm.**

1 Corinthians 10:13 *"But God is faithful to His word and to His compassionate nature, and He can be trusted not to let you be tried beyond your ability and strength of resistance and power to endure; but with the temptation He will always provide the way out, the means of escape to a landing place, that you may be capable and strong and powerful to bear up under it patiently."*
WOW! We need to believe that!

Jesus is always our example and what did He do?
Luke 9: 51: *"He steadfastly and determinedly set His face to go to Jerusalem."*
This is how the eagle embraces the storm and the enemy's plans to destroy him are thwarted as he continues to allow the winds to lift him even higher away from the danger. Storms often come in surprise packages and yet, as we **rejoice**, as we continue to live in an attitude of praise to the God of our salvation.......we will be lifted higher and God takes control and the miracles happen.

The Storm often comes suddenly and very unexpectedly.........seemingly from nowhere:

A good example of exactly this is, when Paul, after many days of excellent ministry, delivers a slave girl from a troubling demon......Just an ordinary day's ministry but suddenly a BIG storm comes from nowhere!
Acts 16: 23-26: *"They threw them into the inner prison and*

fastened their feet in stocks. But about midnight, as Paul and Silas were praying and singing hymns of praise to God, and the other prisoners were listening to them." Paul and Silas embraced the storm as they prayed and sang hymns of praise to God, they did not question, complain or grumble. [although they had that choice!] Instead they embraced the God of their salvation, choosing to see the power of praise work on their behalf, knowing that the Lord was able to set them free. In every storm you need to lean on the Lord and give Him complete control. Drawing near to the Holy Spirit in any stormy situation releases the power of God to work on your behalf.

Then just as quickly, God can step in: "Suddenly there was a great earthquake, so that the foundations of the prison were shaken; and at once the doors were opened and everyone's shackles were unfastened." Obviously, while Paul and Silas were in these stormy conditions, people were watching [others do watch us when we are going through the storms]! In this instance the other prisoners were listening and they saw how Paul and Silas embraced the situation with peace, confidence and faith in the God of their salvation. They watched as God responded to their faith with an earthquake that brought freedom to all of them! Prison doors opened and shackles were unfastened. Liberty is what happens when we are mature enough to retain our peace and faith in God not matter what sudden storm occurs. We can embrace a storm from the enemy, and this will bring freedom, not just for us, but for those in the same storm!

When the Jailer asked: "What is necessary for me to do that I may be saved?" I love Paul's answer: *"Believe in the Lord Jesus Christ, give yourself to Him, take yourself out of your own keeping and you will be saved."* Paul and Silas spread their spiritual wings by faith; praying and praising the Almighty God and look what happened.......**Freedom and liberty, the Gospel was advanced and they all had**

a new perspective beyond the bars of the inner prison, and Glory went to the Living God! That is the exciting life The Holy Spirit has for us when we "Dare to be an Eagle" - the rewards are amazing!

I remember several years ago when we were called to Mallorca. Stepping out had not been easy and there had been some very unexpected storms; and as is often the case, those storms brought some extra gusts of wind that greatly affected us. One of these was the need to sell our house as quickly as possible; but in spite of our doing all that we could do, nothing had moved at all and time was running out fast! I had felt so sure that we would sell to a nurse and yet everyone we approached was not interested. We were being pressed for payment in Mallorca and things did not look good at all in the natural. My husband, as always, was as steady as a rock, standing on God's Word, but I was struggling. The storm clouds were getting at me and instead of stretching my spiritual wings of praise and thanksgiving......all I could see was disaster and loss and what seemed worst of all....God's Name would be laughed at. Yes the enemy was having a field day!

I can still recall that particular day when I wept before the Lord and then how the beautiful Holy Spirit used the Scripture from **Habakkuk 3: 18**: *"Yet, I will rejoice in the God of my salvation."* My husband spoke gently, but firmly with all the authority of God's truth: "Gill, whatever happens, no one can take away your salvation". At that moment, my spirit leapt and my spiritual wings spread, praise erupted from deep within and something broke inside to enable me to embrace the storm and to stop fighting it with my own effort. Just a few days later, God settled things in a completely miraculous way, and yes, we did sell to a nurse from our own church for the exact asking price.....**God intervened on our behalf and it was a complete miracle!**

When we fight the storms instead of embracing them, I personally believe that we can limit God and even delay the breakthrough God has waiting for us. The eagle "sets" his wings at the very first scent of a storm; he has learnt to be ready always to embrace it. Wise bird!

However, the very same eagle has a very different way of dealing with a serpent. **He embraces the storm, but he fights the serpent!** We too need to discern between the storm and the serpent and respond accordingly if we are to be victorious and be all Christ intends us to be. First of all, the eagle sees the serpent as an enemy that is potentially dangerous, one that has to be fought. How do you see the devil? He really is our deadly enemy. Even though a serpent will not attack a full grown eagle, it will try to eat the eggs before they hatch and afterwards the serpent will constantly be a threat to kill and eat the young eaglets still in the nest. Yes, the serpent is the enemy of the eagle, but the eagle has no fear of either the storm or the serpent, he just knows that he must deal with them very differently. We need to be sure that there is no fear in us; if there is, the devil will sense it and attack us even more.

A good example of recognizing the difference between a storm and a serpent is seen with David in the Bible: David would not touch king Saul, God's anointed, even though Saul hounded and persecuted him for years. David had faith in God's word and he knew in his heart what God had said would come true. How often he must have had to remind himself how Samuel had been sent to anoint him to be king. Contentment in God is a sign of embracing a storm and David embraced many storms as he endured the years of persecution in the wilderness. Instead of taking things into his own hands he allowed the years to mature him and he kept his spirit sweet towards Saul in the face of great difficulty.

But how different with Goliath: Goliath was the enemy of Israel [just as the devil is the adversary to all God's people] and David fought and killed him. The eagle knows how to embrace the storm and fight the serpent! We need to learn this! Maybe, even as you have been reading, you are realizing how you have mistakenly fought the storms instead of the enemy. If that is the case, now is the best time to "move on!"

Let us talk to the Holy Spirit together:

Oh Lord, now I can see my mistakes and I really do ask You to forgive me for struggling so much. I repent of all my fleshly reactions that probably prolonged things, when all You wanted to do was to draw me closer to You and lift me up on Your powerful wings. Please help me Holy Spirit, I need You to be my Counsellor every day so that I will learn how to embrace the storms and yet to fight the serpents. Thank You Lord. Amen.

Joseph is another brilliant example: He was rejected, taken, enslaved, imprisoned....BIG storms and yet, God stood back, knowing how these storms would lift Joseph higher and fulfil His purposes for good. Joseph embraced the storms of the hard places, he grew in character, kept a good attitude and God was with him in each stormy situation.

1. The first storm: **Genesis 37:11-24** Joseph's brothers turned against him and left him for dead at the bottom of a well, all because they were jealous and envious of him. Not pleasant at all.....but God was in control.

2. **v27** *"let us sell him to the Midianites....and his brothers consented."* *V36 "the Midianites sold Joseph in Egypt to Potipher an officer of Pharaoh."* But even here, as Joseph was in slavery, we see God's favour was upon him. In other words, whatever the storm it could not stop God's favour and God's Presence or prevent God's purpose for Joseph! That truly is good news!

44

Genesis 39:2 *"And the Lord was with Joseph and he was successful and prosperous, even though he was a slave."*

3. Here is another unexpected storm that blew up from nowhere as Joseph was wrongly accused of immorality....this time ending up in prison.

Genesis 39:1 *"The Hebrew slave whom you brought among us came to me to mock and insult me."* **This was a lie!** How he must have had to fight the serpents trying to get in his mind and thoughts such as: "This is so unfair," "How can I justify myself?" or "Why God did this happen etc?" But instead he embraced the storm, he obviously lived in an on-going forgiving spirit, Joseph moved forward and kept his spirit sweet and again we are told that Joseph found the favour of the Lord even there in prison.

Genesis 39: 21: *"But the Lord was with Joseph and showed him mercy and loving kindness and gave him favour in the sight of the warden of the prison."*

Always beyond a storm is the possibility of a new spiritual level, a new dimension of power and greater freedom, simply because God is in control ALL the time. **Hebrews 11:6** "He is the rewarder of those who diligently seek Him."

Look what happened in the end to Joseph.....

Genesis 41: 14: *"Pharaoh sent and called for him. But first Joseph first shaved himself and changed his clothes and made himself presentable; then he came into Pharaoh's presence."* The great Pharaoh himself sent for Joseph, all because God had created a need that only Joseph's gifts could satisfy! Read the full story for yourself and be amazed how the Lord was in full control ALL the time. The storms were used to prepare Joseph to fulfil his divine destiny and he didn't have to fight them at all! He just embraced the storms in a "right" spirit all the time.

Genesis 41:40-41 *"You shall have charge over my house and all my people shall be governed according to your word...I have set you over all the land of Egypt."*

The eagle embraces the circumstances but fights the serpents that always want to creep in. For us, they are the little foxes, the hidden serpents that rise up on the inside of us feeding on our flesh that can never reflect the Christ-like nature. We need to identify these spiritual serpents such as:

Anger, frustration, rebellion, resentment and all attitudes of offence - unforgiveness and bitterness to name but a few!

Joseph embraced the storms but fought those serpents that could have killed him as they did kill Saul.

We must fight these serpents with all that is within us. If we don't, these serpents will kill us quicker than any storm. The eagle has learnt to be wise and fearless in dealing with these serpents and it depends on his ability to **swoop down at about 200 mph!**

1 John 4: 18: *"Perfect love casts out ALL fear."* We must deal with any roots of fear!

The eagle swoops down to snatch the offending serpent in his long, sharp talons, just as it is about to kill the young eaglets or eat the vulnerable eggs before they are hatched. The eagle is alert to the danger and uses his ability to swoop on his enemy and kill it.

He does one of two things:

1. Having caught the serpent, the eagle flies high above the highest rock and literally throws the alive, wriggling and struggling serpent down on to the rock where it is smashed to death in pieces.

WOW! What a wonderful example to us:

We too, need to recognise these spiritual serpents like irritation, self-pity or even taking offence, these are able to burst in unexpectedly and harm us.....We should quickly realize what has happened and be active in fighting against them. Spiritually we need to **"GRAB" whatever you may sense is trying to get in, and fly to the Lord of Glory!** Confess how you feel and cast it upon the Rock Christ Jesus. Let Him deal with it; He did it all at the cross 2000 years ago. Jesus' victory is complete, once and for all; no serpent can live in the sight of the cross or survive the blood of the Lamb. Don't waste time wondering what to do, **"swoop down" and use your spiritual talons of all authority and power over the enemy.**

Luke 10: 19: *"Behold! I have given you authority and power to trample upon serpents and scorpions, and physical and mental strength and ability over all the power that the enemy possesses; and nothing shall in any way harm you."* The eagle watches to see that the serpent is dead and hovers above it in delight knowing that his enemy is smashed and will never trouble him again!

2. If the eagle catches the serpent approaching where the eggs are, or where the young eaglets are in the nest, he again **swoops down**, grasps the offending serpent in his talons and takes it to the nearest high rock where the Eagle slices off its dangerous head with its sharp beak and then proceeds to feed the body to the young eaglets! **Yes, eagles eat snakes!** Learning to fight serpents can only build you up and help you grow, so you can be all you are meant to be in Christ. Never be afraid of the enemy, spiritually behead them at the cross and render them harmless, so they will not hurt you or others. The eagle knows when to embrace the storm and when to fight the serpent; both depend on his ability to use his wings in two different ways.

NEVER EMBRACE A SERPENT, you can't afford to ignore it either, because it will hurt you....**fight it!**

EMBRACE THE STORM and it will take you to a new level in Christ.

Chapter Five

FLYING TO FRUITFULNESS

"Mount up close to God as eagles mount up to the sun."
Isaiah 40:31

One of the most important things that God is saying to His Body in these days is all about **'Intimacy'**. I love this interpretation **"Into-me-u-see!"** Yes, intimacy means nothing is hidden, absolute oneness, true partnership, complete transparency and vulnerability. That is real intimate relationship. I have come to find that that is what we have been created for, and I believe that the eagle has much to teach us, if we will allow him.

Being **close to God** has to be in the heavenly realms, it is impossible to be close to God in the flesh because God is Spirit!

Ephesians 2: 6: *"He raised us up together with Him and made us sit down together, giving us joint seating with Him in the heavenly places."* To make this possible The Messiah Himself our Saviour came to earth as the Man Christ Jesus, He came to reveal the Father to us. **1 John 3:5** *"He appeared in visible form and became Man to take away upon Himself our sins, and in Him there was no sin."* **Romans 5:7-8 The Message** *"God put His love on the line for us by offering His Son....while we were of no use whatever to Him."*......... At Calvary, Jesus stood between God's anger and the punishment for our sins. Having lived the life we couldn't live, then He took the punishment we couldn't escape and now He freely offers us redemption we couldn't afford. WHAT A SAVIOUR!
Acts 2:23-24 *"This Jesus when delivered up according to the definite and fixed purpose of God, you crucified.......But God*

49

raised Him up, liberating Him from the pangs of death." And He will be coming back again, the Bible says so!

Acts 1:11 *"This same Jesus will return in just the same way in which you saw Him go into heaven."* The disciples had just seen Jesus caught up in a cloud and carried Him away out of their sight. Before he went, Jesus made this astounding promise....

Acts 1:8 *"You shall receive power, ability, efficiency and might when the Holy Spirit has come on you......"*

When Jesus had completed His earthly mission, He sent God, The Holy Spirit [as He promised] to "in-dwell" believers. **NOW to-day,** He is here to enable us to have that unique relationship of **Friendship with the Holy Spirit, as Lover with the Lord Jesus and as that special Father-Child** intimacy when we mount up close to God Himself. Many of us find this depth of intimacy very threatening because we feel ashamed or exposed; a bit like Adam and Eve who tried to cover their nakedness with fig leaves! It was never meant to be this way, only sin brings shame, and we need to remember that God sees us as spotless..... 'washed in the blood of His beloved Son' The Bible says: **Galatians 3: 27:** *"Clothe yourself with Christ."*

Psalm 91: 4: *"He will cover you with His wings."* So I pray, that you and I will learn from the eagle and know that you are safe in His arms and He is just waiting to share Himself with you.

Paul longed for this - **Philippians 3: 9-10:** *"That I may actually be found and known as in Him....For my determined purpose is that I may know Him....and in that same way come to know the power out flowing from His resurrection."*

The Word 'KNOW' in the Greek is 'Ginomai,' meaning 'Become as one.' In the Hebrew, "Yada", meaning 'Seen as one.' Yada refers to the ultimate intimacy between a man and a woman and that they may be fruitful. This is the same word Yada in:

1 Samuel 1: 19: *"Elkanah **knew** Hannah his wife; and the Lord remembered her and Hannah became pregnant."* God has always ordained fruitfulness; as we see in

Genesis 2: 28: *"Go forth and multiply and be fruitful."* And today, this is still God's purpose for us to be fruitful. He has created us for intimacy with Himself which, in turn always results in fruitfulness to His Glory.

John15:16 Jesus said, *"You have not chosen Me, but I have chosen you and I have appointed you, that you might go and bear fruit and keep on bearing, and that your fruit may be lasting...."*

We can draw a comparison with our spiritual development to that of the young eagle.

At first he does his own thing; he is not ready for that depth of loyalty, commitment and intimacy of relationship. Then for one to three years he will fly high and independently, he will fly far and wide, all the time gaining experience and strength and learning how to feed and defend himself. All of this time, the young immature eagle, with all his potential, will live a mainly independent and irresponsible lifestyle....selfishly only considering himself and enjoying it!! I suppose you would you call him "fancy free" from all responsibilities!

I wonder if you remember how it was with you when you were first saved? How you would rush from one meeting to another, how you simply must hear a certain speaker, or buy that particular Tape/CD everyone is talking about.....All the time so "hungry"....but really doing what seemed wise in your own eyes. Yes, **immature and passionate** and yet full of the zeal of the Lord! Often, I have found that it was in those impressionable, immature days that the enemy made sure many young Christians got badly wounded, misunderstood and even isolated. Church situations 'blew up', people who were thought to be pillars in the church suddenly fell into sin; and hurts happened. Some, may be you, decided you didn't need a church, but would love the

Lord in your own way....too hurt to risk opening up yourself again. However, whatever happened and how you came through it, will have left marks, or even maybe scars, that need healing. Though you may resist it, what you need is **more intimacy, not less!** I sense in the Holy Spirit that that may be you, if so let's move on together and allow the beautiful Holy Spirit to bring healing to those buried hurts. **Let us pray together:**

Father, in Jesus' Name I come to You, yes things did happen in those early days and I didn't understand what was going on, nor how vulnerable I was. I confess that there are wounds and I decided not to trust people again. Please Lord forgive me for closing myself up, I was afraid that I would be rejected, when all the time You had been rejected in my place on the cross. Lord God send Your healing Holy Spirit to turn my scars into stars that will shine for You....Thank You Lord Amen.

Now let us find out what the eagle does! He has enjoyed his so called freedom and independence.....UNTIL one day he sees a beautiful female eagle who is out to get his attention! She flies with effortless ease in a very large 'figure of eight' pretending to be oblivious of her male admirer. The young male eagle decides to follow her as she flies in her figure of eight. Now for the first time **he is no longer flying his own path**, love is drawing him into a different pattern of flight. This is exactly what happens to us as we soar in the Spirit up close to the Lord, we come to experience the incredible love the Father has for us:

1 John 3: 1: *"See what an incredible love the Father has bestowed on us that we should be permitted to be called the children of God! And so we are!"*

It has to be **the love of God** that draws us away from our own independent lifestyle and self-centredness. His special unconditional love that covers a multitude of sins, this incredible holy love that always draws us closer, will keep us away from temptation and even bad company...His love is so strong that we will want His will and His Kingdom before our own comfort or our own desires. Only God's love can really do this as we are empowered by His Spirit! **Romans 5:5** *"For God's love has been poured out in our hearts through the Holy Spirit Who has been given to us."*

One example comes to mind. It was shortly after the New Year several years ago. A young Christian man had been involved in a very nasty bicycle accident, going into the rear of the car in front of him because his anorak hood blew over his face. He was certainly fortunate to be alive as he had sustained terrible head and facial injuries and had been moved to the special unit in Swansea Hospital for surgery the next day. I was earnestly praying for him on this particular morning, when God's love poured into my heart for him and the Holy Spirit whispered, "Go and lay hands on him, I am going to heal him through you." At the same time, this Scripture bounced into my spirit: **Malachi 4: 2:** *"The sun of righteousness will rise with healing in his wings."* Part of me was excited, while the human side groaned! As I was due in work, I rang my unsaved boss, honestly thinking he would call me straight into work; but he didn't, instead he told me to go straight to Swansea. Wow! Here was the Spirit of God going before me..... So with much trembling I set off. I was no longer flying my own path but I was definitely following The Spirit on the Lord's business. Amazingly, I was allowed in to see him. His jaw was wired ready to be broken and then re-set, so he couldn't speak, but I did notice that he had his Bible open on the bed. I glanced and saw **Malachi 4: 2:** *"The sun of righteousness will rise with healing in his wings."* Yes, the very same scripture that the Spirit had quickened to me! My spirit leapt as God confirmed His Word. I hastily laid hands on him, prayed in the Spirit and ran!

My point is this; that suddenly I was no longer on my own path. This was God's idea, I felt very inadequate, weak and fearful but for the first time, out of my obedience...came the blessing of healing for this young man. Apparently when they got him to theatre, they found that the jaw had miraculously been completely restored by God and no further surgery was necessary! Fruitfulness comes from obedience.

There must come a time in our lives when we cease to do our own thing and decide to be about our Heavenly Father's business, serving His purposes obediently in our generation......just like Jesus:
Luke 2: 49: *"Did you not know it was necessary for Me to be about My Father's business?"* I would love to say from that moment I have never wandered off onto my own path but that would not be true. It is a journey, a process of learning to follow the Spirit day by day, walking in tune with Him. For me, the most important thing is that the path we fly should be motivated by this deep **'love relationship'** with the Lord Himself. If not, we shall find ourselves moving into striving and works of the flesh and wonder where the Grace has gone. I always think of the 'eagle's wings' that enable us to soar as being the abounding Grace that will not let me go. Fruitfulness is always initiated by the Holy Spirit!

The young eagle is happy to play 'Tag' with the female eagle. As soon as she knows he is really interested, she swoops down and picks up a small twig and soars to about 10,000 feet and drops it. Screeching wildly at him, she conveys that he is expected to catch it before it hits the ground. He is more than happy to show off his prowess and does it easily, carrying it back to her...only to find that she completely ignores him! Instead, back she goes to get another branch and repeats this whole procedure. Each time she releases a larger branch at a lower height so that it gets more and more difficult for the young male eagle to get it before it touches the ground! Finally she collects the biggest branch she can manage, flies to only 500 feet and lets it fall fast towards the ground. Now if he is finally successful with this large branch, and only then, will they move into real courtship. Should he fail, she will immediately fly off and is no longer interested in a life-long relationship!

What is this all about? The female eagle is looking for a mate for life, she wants quality, perseverance, strength and ability; she is looking for his attitude of service and ability to look after her.

Is it possible? Could God be looking for such things in us? I believe that the answer is YES! He needs to know our loyalty, how mature we are and whether we will persevere or give up easily when things get tough. He will check our attitudes in adverse conditions, He will notice how obedient and faithful we have become and watch for the servant heart like His own Son.

In other words, **God is looking for commitment,** so He can use us to fulfil His purposes and release His power through us and see us reach our potential. **Intimacy is all about God, the Holy Spirit, sharing Himself with us and us** proving our trustworthiness to soar close to Him.

Once the young female eagle is satisfied that he is the best for her, she will rise up high into the sky and almost without warning, "screeching" she flops over on her back, folds her wings, puts out her talons and "free falls" to certain death unless something intervenes. The male eagle hears and sees and he swoops at a top speed of 200 mph, spreads his wings and locks his talons onto hers. At this point he takes all her weight, supports her under his wings and they become one. Gently falling together, they consummate the beginning of their life-long partnership to the death and apparently they even sing a love song as they are united in intimacy.

Can you see the spiritual revelation of this picture? How God Himself longs to hear us cry to Him and yearns for us to need Him with all our being in absolute sweet surrender. It is at this point that we will finally come to know, that ONLY IN HIM is Life, Hope, Purpose and Fulfilment and that **now we understand** what it means to say - **Jesus is Lord of all**. At last we have come to be utterly dependent on Him, enjoying the new found intimacy where He is in full control...not us! We grow into this beautiful dependency as we surrender to the Holy Spirit.

This total **dependency and surrender is something we give to the Lord. It is our love-gift to Him as a response to Calvary.**
It is simply because of our love relationship with our Saviour the Lord Jesus Christ, it is an act of our heart and spirit and will never be something He will ever demand from us. But I believe it thrills His heart when he finds hearts like this and with it will come true intimacy and real fruitfulness. Only a few years ago, I found myself yearning for greater intimacy and I somehow knew the secret lay in my greater dependency on Him; so I prayed a simple prayer for the Holy Spirit to bring me to a new depth of dependency on Him. I forgot, but God never forgets our prayers and always answers in His way and at His time! It was a short heart-felt prayer which you too can pray if you want to....

Holy Spirit I know I want to have a deeper and more intimate relationship with you. Will You make me more dependent on You?...Thank You Lord. Amen.

Several months later it was a very hot, sultry summer

day in Mallorca where I live. I was on my way hom   lo
praying hard for the elusive parking place. I was thrille   th
so grateful to the Lord to see an ideal parking place ri   d
front of our home! As is usually my way, I prepared to re   tl
into the space [after all I have been driving for almo   V
years, so this was no problem!?] but I missed it and h   t
curb, only to try again. After three attempts I distinctly l   y
the Holy Spirit say, "Would you like Me to help you   r
didn't actually answer, but my attitude was, "No thank y   ▪
can do it fine." I continued to try and park for anothe   :
times without any success. By now I was sweating profu
I was agitated and my peace had flown out the window
ago. Again I heard the Holy Spirit say, "Would you like
to help you?" Very disgruntled, I spoke aloud, "Oh OK!" /
yes, I reversed in to the parking place perfectly with
difficulty at all. Then it suddenly occurred to me to ask
Holy Spirit, "What was that all about?" What He s
absolutely shocked me and utterly changed my life for ev
"Gill, if I withdraw My grace from any part of your life y
will never succeed at anything; from now on you will not
able to park a car without asking Me for help, you will
utterly dependent on Me." It hit me like a bombshe
Suddenly I remembered my prayer and I could see for tl
first time, that without God I could do nothing:

John 15: 5:   *"Apart from Me you can do nothing."* To this d
it is true; I always need to ask for help from the Holy Spir
in parking the car. Occasionally I forget and hit the curb o
even the car in front or behind....how I quickly repent an
move forward into my dependency on the Spirit of God!

Earlier in my Christian walk, I found it more difficult
to relate to God intimately as my Father. I realized that there
must be a 'blockage' from my background, so once again I
asked the Holy Spirit to reveal what was the hindrance. Very
quickly the Spirit reminded me of my own father, whom I

ed greatly. All through my childhood, he had promised
ngs but was obviously unable to keep his word for many
ferent reasons. Somehow I had subconsciously transferred
s to my Heavenly Father. I believed His promises in the
rd would be fulfiled for others, but I found it so hard to
ieve for me because I saw myself as not good enough. Can
u see how the devil had deceived me, because of bad
gative things that had affected my relationship with my own
tural father?.....This was exactly what the devil used to rob
e of that intimate, special relationship with my Heavenly
ther. I quickly repented and forgave my own father and
en knew the wonderful restoring hand of a loving Father as
e caressed me as His child and brought healing into those
amaged emotions. Maybe you too have experienced a less
an perfect human father, perhaps in an abusive situation
here your own natural father demonstrated his love to you
a forbidden sexual way? Or in another way that can be
qually damaging such as a cold remoteness that hurts so
uch when you just long for your daddy's arms to cuddle
ou. I meet so many who have never experienced a normal
ving relationship with their human fathers, and the result is
hat they find it so hard to have a secure intimate relationship
with anyone, let alone God their Heavenly Father. It is SO
ad and I know, a little, how the Holy Spirit is grieved because
he enemy has robbed so many in the Body of Christ of real
ntimacy. But the Good News is there for everyone, praise
God for every situation there is a Redeemer...His Name is
Jesus! Cruelty too, that no one knows about, also stifles our
intimacy with God; and can give us a hard time trusting God
that He is ALWAYS GOOD. I want to tell you, the Holy
Spirit does care and He knows all about everything and He
longs to bring you His comfort and help as you open up to
Him. Sometimes this is so painful it is even hard to face up
to the truth, but the Holy Spirit brings courage to even the
faint hearted if you will allow Him....

Make this your prayer and see how gently He will come to you:

Holy Spirit You know all the hidden issues that are hindering me from going deeper in an intimate relationship with You...I so want to be fruitful for You. Help me and set me free in the Name of Jesus Amen.

Perhaps it would be good to look again at how the eagle can teach us.... No one can save her from certain death as she "free falls" towards the earth, only the male eagle has the ability to save her and he responds immediately he hears her cry; she totally depends on him and he will not let her go.

Know that the Divine Eagle has heard your cry and He comes to commit Himself to you for now and all eternity. The Father Himself cherishes you, He is the perfect Father and He will not let you go, never, never, never! That is His absolute commitment to you, which He proved by sending His own Son to be the perfect sacrifice for you at Calvary.

Jeremiah 31: 3: *"Yes, I have loved you with an everlasting love."* Hear the Lord singing over you:

Zephaniah 3: 17: *"He will exult over you with singing."* His own love song to you!

Some people find this depth of intimacy a bit overpowering. But for me, I have found it to be both liberating and fulfiling. As you will allow the Holy Spirit to come into those hurting, hidden places He will give you the precious intimacy you and He so greatly desires. This is total dependency and real intimacy which so pleases God our Father and it always produces the fruitfulness we all long for in our lives as we fly His path and not our own.

Chapter Six

RENEWED AS AN EAGLE

"Your youth, renewed, is like the eagle's."
Psalm 103:5

The Bible has several scriptures about being renewed and these often refer to the eagle. I have found that there are some wonderful hidden revelations to be explored as I have studied how the eagle is renewed.

Psalm103:5 The Message: *"He renews your youth; you are always young in His Presence."* I love that particular translation, because it always encourages me about the benefits of being in His Presence. It should encourage you too!

Isaiah 40:31 *"They shall renew their strength and power as an eagle."* Many times I have needed more strength and power and I always find it in His Word and in His Presence! This is a promise from the Word of God that is for you.

The Dictionary says: Renew means to make new again, to restore to the original, make fresh and vigorous again and to make as good as new!

Strong's Concordance says: To rebuild, to repair, to restore!

Recently I was asked to speak at a Conference on the theme of "Restoration." I had studied for several days and yet in spite of all the good things I still felt that something was missing. The following day, I just happened to be sitting next to one of the leaders in a church I was visiting and asked him casually if he knew anything about restoration. Almost to my amazement, he said he didn't, but he had a friend who was a master craftsman in the restoration of old furniture. Later that day I was thrilled to speak to this man, and although I have never met him, I am indebted to him for these treasures he shared with me about restoration.

Firstly he told me that there can be no restoration on anything that is not valuable. Wow! I was so excited when I realized that our wonderful Father God, Who is the Master Craftsman in all restoration and renewal, is more than willing to work on us.....Just because we are SO VALUABLE to Him!

Next the gentleman shared how a master craftsman has three objectives:

a] To change as little as possible.
b] That it must function as it was intended.
c] To renew and restore it to its original purpose.

I was beginning to see how God, Who created us, had one aim to make us like His own Son Jesus Christ! However, then he shared the most astounding fact of all..... He told me that on the most priceless pieces of furniture, there are often damages that have happened over the years, but these marks are left and highly polished as they add to the value! Can you see the spiritual revelation? The very wounds, the hurtful things that have bruised our lives and have left marks, can actually enhance our value and reflect our Maker to an even greater degree than before! In fact I can say that often these very things can be the pivotal point of release in ministry. I am sharing this because I really don't want you to resist being renewed or restored; respond quickly, it could be the key you have been waiting for!

In our busy lives, most of us have experienced times of weariness or even dryness in our spiritual walk with the Lord. Sometimes just **'soaking'** in His presence is sufficient and refreshes us as we pass through that particular season. However, there are other times when it may seem like a really prolonged wilderness. This is when we need to remember that God often does some of His deepest work at these times. It happened to Moses and the young lover in Song of Songs, so it can happen to us!

Hosea 2: 14: *"Behold I will allure her to bring her into the wilderness and I will speak tenderly to her."* I so want you to know that the wilderness is not necessarily a negative place, especially for those that love God. As we look in the Bible, every great person of God went through a wilderness time, yes even Jesus, every so often it was there that they heard the call of God on their lives. Do you remember Moses? He desperately needed renewing after his flight from Egypt in disgrace for murder. The Bible tells us how it happened:

Exodus 3:1-2 He was in the back-side of the wilderness, where he'd been for 40 years tending sheep......[Oh help us Lord not to keep You waiting!] Then one ordinary day, as he watched over the sheep, something caught his attention; .... a burning bush that didn't burn up! Suddenly the Angel of the Lord appeared to him and spoke to him personally, in what appears to be the first time in forty years. Here comes the "call" of God to Moses!

Exodus 3:10 "Come now I will send you to Pharaoh, that you may bring My people out of Egypt" The wilderness became the "meeting place" with God for Moses. For us too, it can be a place where new revelation comes, a place of commission and a place of deep lasting renewal and restoration as it was with Moses.

So what is a wilderness?
I believe that the Holy Spirit has given me this definition:
a] Somewhere you would rather not be.
b] Something you would rather not have.

God's people have always experienced wildernesses and I guess they will continue to; so we need desperately to learn how to be renewed as the eagle. We should learn to allow the Holy Spirit to use these times to the maximum and be reminded how He led His people, Israel, into and through the wilderness for 40 years.

Deuteronomy 8: 2: *"How the Lord led you in the wilderness, to humble you and to prove you."* When you find yourself in the wilderness, you need to remember that it is never a time when you are forgotten and ignored by God, nor is it a place of defeat. Often it is an opportunity where the hidden depth of our hearts are revealed to us, [of course the Holy Spirit already knows what is there] but we need to know so that we can humble ourselves in His Presence and receive from His storehouse of mercy, grace and ever-transforming love!

I still remember vividly one of my wilderness times. I had done everything I knew how to get myself out of this desert period, but nothing worked! I had repented, read the Word, worshipped, prayed for extended times in "tongues" and even fasted and spent extra time alone with the Lord...... but still it was as if the heavens were as brass! Eventually, I literally "spread-eagled" myself before the Lord and said, "Lord I've done everything I know how to be close to you and nothing works, now You will have to do it because Lord I don't know what is wrong with me!" I was utterly amazed that instantly the Holy Spirit clearly spoke to me, but it was especially what He said that shocked me and changed my life forever. He said, "Gill, thank goodness you have stopped trying, you are a million times worse than you think AND I LOVE YOU!" Some people may think that was not good news, but I knew some things that were not right and if I was a million times worse and STILL he loved me......then that was WONDERFUL news!!!! Instantly praise and tears of joy erupted from deep within me, there and then I was renewed and restored and found myself swimming in the river of His merciful love! In a moment God can change everything!

2 Corinthians 2: 14: *"Christ always leads us in triumph."*

The wilderness can definitely be a season of renewing, restoration and rebuilding and even re-alignment. How you respond to the Holy Spirit while you are in the wilderness, will determine how you come out. It should always make you more confident of Who God is to you personally and who you are in Christ. You will be refreshed, restored and you will have more strength. Always, as He renews you, you will be overwhelmed at His incredible love, mercy and grace. It is this revelation that will enable you to be more than a conqueror so that you will be able to soar as the eagle! The wilderness can be God's precious gift of real renewal and restoration to you!

Song of Songs 8: 5: *"Who is this who comes up from the wilderness leaning on her Beloved?"*

Desert periods in our lives are opportunities to be drawn closer to Jesus. You might not be able to understand it at the time but God always has a higher purpose than you can imagine! If you could see and understand it, you would get in the way and try to help God out,[or at least I would!] instead of allowing the Holy Spirit to do His work, which He does so beautifully. Even inner spiritual dryness is a time of potential new revelation as you yield to the Spirit. When you 'feel' nothingness, seem to be 'stripped' of all your resources, feel let down, empty, lonely, oppressed, weak, helpless and hopeless, or downright hurt, disappointed or full of pain and grief ....Then there are promises for you in the Bible.

Isaiah 51: 3 *"He will comfort all the waste places and He will make the wilderness like Eden and her desert like the garden of the Lord."* Perhaps that is you right now and God has brought this book into your hands to bring you hope....I want to assure you that the Holy Spirit is your Comforter and however you are feeling, or whatever are the circumstances, **HE WILL COME TO YOU** with His special love and peace as you open up before Him in complete honesty.

Please let me pray for you this time..... Lord Jesus, You said, that You would ask the Father and that He would send another Comforter to remain with us forever; now Lord I am asking that You fulfil this promise for Your precious hurting child and let Yourself be clearly seen and make Yourself known in a very real and personal way. Give hope where there seems to be no hope, give love where there seems to be no love and Lord, bring answers where they are desperately needed. Thank You Holy Spirit that you anointed Jesus to heal the broken-hearted and You are still doing it today to the Glory of God the Father Amen.

Being renewed is for ALL of us, if we recognize our need for it. We can ALL receive the joy of renewal and restoration experiencing the times of refreshing that the Lord has for us in His Presence: The Bible says:

Acts 3: 19: *"Repent, Return to God that times of refreshing may come from the Presence of the Lord."* David experienced this. I wonder how many times he must have watched the eagle in the wilderness as he lived and hid from Saul, and how he came to understand so well, what it meant to be renewed as the eagle. David said these words just after he had fallen into sin with Bathsheba:

Psalm 51: 10: *"Renew a right persevering and steadfast spirit in me O Lord."*

Or the same scripture in The Message says: *"Put fresh wind in my sails."*

Jesus too, spoke about refreshment:

Matthew 11: 28: *"Come to Me and I will refresh you."* Jesus understood that we need renewing and showed us how we will experience it if we come to Him.

How does the Eagle get renewed?

1. **He recognises his need:** In time, the eagle's feathers get

worn or damaged. The result is that they don't work as they should and so he gets slower when he swoops down to catch his prey. At the same time, the worn feathers begin to make a high-pitched whistling noise as he dives down to catch his prey; this sound alerts the prey so that catching the prey becomes much more difficult and the eagle can begin to go hungry.

How does this apply to our spiritual lives?

Praise and worship are food to our spirit, but sometimes our 'spiritual feathers' get worn and tired, so praise and worship can seem less important. Do you know how I notice it? My husband and I worship and pray together each morning, but at times the pressures of life push that time out of the picture and suddenly we realize that our depth of closeness has been stolen and we need renewing!

2. **The eagle realizes that his vision is not as sharp as it was** and his focus can be distracted.

How does this apply to our spiritual lives?

When we need renewing, we too are less spiritually alert, maybe we could even miss the quiet gentle voice of the Holy Spirit. We can also become dull in perceiving how the enemy is trying to creep into our lives with distractions and busyness!

3. **The talons of the eagle have become blunt** and his beak has built up with calcification; so he is less able to grip his prey and finds it hard to tear the flesh apart to feed himself or his young

How does this apply to our spiritual lives?

We need to be able to spiritually 'discern' situations in our lives, to live an overcoming life. One of the most important things is our mouth...... it is possible that we might have begun to speak negatively, or just neglecting to positively proclaim God's Word? These things creep in almost without us realizing. I have said before, that what we say, gives permission to the enemy to bring negative things into our lives. So we need to be constantly checking that our mouths have not been infiltrated and affected by the world around us to criticise, judge or gossip about people. Deal with your mouth and be renewed as the eagle.

4. **Now the eagle knows he needs to be renewed.....**so he flies to the highest rock to get as close to the sun as he can, just as he always does! He sits on the rock, ignores the pain and **proceeds to pull out** all the damaged or broken feathers, sometimes as many as 7000 feathers! He is quite ruthless, not prepared to leave one that is broken or damaged! **Micah 1: 6:** *"Enlarge your baldness as the eagle."* The Bible tells us that the eagle can even become bald to prepare for the new growth!

Applying this spiritual principle depends on the quality of our renewal: Being bald as an eagle speaks to me of becoming transparent and vulnerable before a holy God; we need never be afraid of this as I have discovered it to be the very safest of places! But we do need to be ruthless in stopping all fleshly activity, cut off all wrong relationships and deal with the root of sin....ready to be renewed. That is our responsibility!

5. **Then the eagle flies up even higher to find the source of a mountain stream.**
It has to be clear, cool and powerfully gushing over the rock......He then rolls continually over and over in the sparkling water washing off all the parasites that have tried to live on him. At the same time the fresh water stings and stimulates new growth!
How should we apply this to our spiritual lives?
We need to get into the Manifest Presence of God, take time

and stay there and allow Him to cleanse us in the hidden places. He will renew and restore us with His Spirit so that we will become more and more fruitful as we bask in the Glory of His Love, bathe in His Generosity, Mercy and Grace.

Psalm 16:11 *"In Your presence is fullness of joy, at Your right hand there are pleasures for evermore."*

6. Now the eagle "waits" and "fasts" in the sun for up to 40 days.....

This is because he has repeatedly knocked his beak against the rock to get rid of the calcification and to sharpen it, so he stays there fasting! While he waits, he also sharpens his talons on the rock. The eagle is doing his part to prepare for his renewal, while God makes the miracle of new growth!

This final Application to our lives is the most important of all: 'Waiting' in God's Presence is not wasted time. We need to co-operate with the Spirit as He begins to reveal things to you:

a] Negate in Jesus' Name all of your own negative words and any others that people have spoken over you.

b] Confess the Word over yourself.

c] Forgive as He has forgiven you in Christ, especially forgive yourself and maybe even God when you have blamed Him!

d] Worship the Lord in the beauty of Holiness.

Psalm 95: 1-2 *'Let us make a joyful noise to the Lord. O come let us sing to Rock of our salvation. Let us come before His Presence with thanksgiving."*

e] Pray in the Holy Spirit in your heavenly love language of "Tongues."

Jude 22-23 *"You beloved, build yourselves upon your most holy faith [make progress, rise like an edifice higher and higher], praying in the Holy Spirit. Guard and keep yourselves in the love of God."*

7. The eagle also has a daily renewal:

This is far less extreme but just as necessary for his well-being. Each day before he does anything or goes anywhere, he spends at least an hour 'preening' himself. What he does, is to actually breathe onto each individual feather and from a small gland in his mouth, he secrets oil that waterproofs the feathers so he will be able to fly in all weather conditions

Applying this principle is so wonderful!

Oh what a glorious picture for us to remember as we seek the Lord early each morning, before the pressures and events of each day come bursting in. Spending a time of devotion with the Holy Spirit will permit Him to breathe on us His holy anointing oil as we worship and adore our Lord. This will enable us to 'fly' above the storms, no matter what happens during the day. The oil represents the Holy Spirit and His anointing that is within us.

1 John 2: 27 *"The anointing which you received from Him abides permanently in you."*

Ephesians 4: 23 *"Be constantly renewed in the spirit of your mind, having a fresh mental and spiritual attitude."* Be renewed in your heart so that you always remain soft and responsive to His love. This is a very real personal prayer that I ask almost every day...Please Lord do not allow my heart to get calloused or hard. I suppose I ask this so urgently because I know that for me it is always a possibility that it could happen and sometimes does!

Maybe you would just like to speak that as your prayer right now? "Lord please keep my heart soft to You and to others in Jesus' Name I pray Amen."

Ephesians 6: 11 *"Put on God's armour that you may be able successfully to stand up against all the strategies and deceits of the devil."* Make sure that you are covered in the precious blood of Jesus as you wear His armour daily.

If the eagle has a time of renewal each day, how much more should we spend time too?

Psalm 91: 1 *"Dwell in the secret place of the Most High, there we*

*shall remain stable and fixed under the shadow of the Almighty,
whose power no foe can withstand."* Being renewed as the eagle
is vital if we are to avoid 'crash landings' when the unexpected
storms arise out of nowhere. Job speaks of the eagle –

Job 39: 28 *"On the cliff he dwells and remains securely; upon the
point of the rock and the stronghold."*

John 5: 17 Jesus says, *"My Father is always at His work to this
very day and I, too, am working."*

Psalm 103: 5 The Message says, *"He puts victims back on their
feet. God will bring justice back in our lives."* Yes, the Holy Spirit
renews victims of society; God knows how you have been
treated unfairly and He has restoration and renewal for you.
Be sure that you do your part.....**Forgive!**

R.T. Kendall writes: "It is no spiritual victory to think
we are forgiving, when we are only avoiding facing up to
wrong behaviour. We are saying ...I want to forgive them,
but I don't think I could if they actually did what it seems
they did. So be careful of postponing recognition of the real
offence to avoid feeling the pain. **Total forgiveness is
painful.** It hurts to kiss revenge goodbye. It hurts to think
that the person is getting away with what they did and that
nobody will ever find out. But when we know fully what they
did and accept in our hearts that they will be blessed without
any consequences imposed by us....then we cross over into
the spiritual realm and begin to be a little more like Jesus."
Hallelujah, it is possible!

Genesis 45:1 That was what Joseph did when he sent
everyone out before speaking to his brothers after 22
years...he covered their sin! This is how God puts victims
back on their feet, how He vindicates and restores and
redeems through the blood of the cross.

Such an instance occurred several years ago which is
a good example and it made me realize this principle of
renewal to a higher degree. I was working as a Care Assistant
in a wonderful strict Jewish Home for the elderly. My

colleague, who worked alongside me, hated me for no apparent reason and I became a victim of abuse and lies. My husband and I prayed much about the situation, but it seemed the more we prayed the worse it got! Yes it was a most painful time. Eventually it came to light that the reason she hated me was because I reminded her of her best friend who had died of cancer in spite of trusting God for healing. Her hatred was not really against me at all, but against God whom I loved and she blamed! When I realized that my joyfulness and my happy countenance was reflecting Jesus to the point where she could hardly restrain herself from physically attacking me, I felt a surge of pride, pleased with the way I was handling this very difficult situation.........UNTIL....in my own time of devotion, The Holy Spirit showed me how He viewed it:

Psalm 131:1 *"Lord my heart is not haughty....."* Immediately I was cut to the core of my being as I saw my own spiritual pride and how it was so obnoxious to the Lord. I quickly repented and recalled David's words.

Psalm 51: 10-12 *"Create in me a clean heart, O God, and* **renew** *a right spirit with in me. Cast me not away from your presence and take not your Holy Spirit from me. Restore to me the joy of your salvation and uphold me with a willing spirit."*

Psalm 61:1-2 *"Hear my cry , O God; listen to my prayer. From the end of the earth will I cry to You, when my heart is overwhelmed and fainting; lead me to the rock that is higher than I."*

I too, needed to come to the Rock to be renewed; it was painful to confess my spiritual pride but oh so glorious! I asked for help from the Helper Himself and there began almost 18 months of thinking, speaking and confessing that this woman was my best friend. Love poured into my heart for her from the Holy Spirit.

Romans 5: 5 *"For God's love has been poured out in our hearts through the Holy Spirit."* Gradually things changed, but most of all I changed! On the day I left that employment, she stood

71

before everyone to give me a leaving present and said, "I want to say that Gill has been the best friend anyone could have had!" That brought Glory to the Lord!

Perhaps you have a situation where you feel that you are being victimized, make sure, above everything else, that your spirit has no bitterness, resentment or hidden anger against people.

Ephesians 6:12 *"For we are not wrestling with flesh and blood."* Forgive and trust everything into the hands of your loving Heavenly Father, that was what Jesus chose to do!

1 Peter 2:23 *"When He[Jesus] was reviled and insulted, He did not revile or offer insult in return; He made no threats of vengeance; but He trusted Himself and everything to Him Who judges fairly."* My prayer for you is simply that you draw as close as possible to the Lord, allow Him to renew and restore you and then "wait expectantly" to see what the Holy Spirit will miraculously do about the situation. He will probably completely surprise you!

This will be the sort of living example that demonstrates the power of being renewed and it always brings the Glory to God and not to people! Oh the tremendous miracle of being restored.....it affects, not only us, but those around us! God certainly puts victims back on their feet and He will bring justice back into our lives **if we are renewed as the eagle**.

Chapter Seven

SEEING BEYOND

"On the cliffs he [the eagle] dwells...from there he spies out the prey; and his eyes see it afar off."
Job 39:28-29

Deuteronomy 32:10 *"He scanned him, [penetratingly] he kept him as the pupil of his eye.....as an eagle."*

Starting with Jesus is always the most excellent place! Jesus only did what He **saw** the Father doing:

John 5: 19 *"He is able to do only what He sees the Father doing."* That is what Jesus said of Himself.

The Greek word here is 'Optomai' meaning to gaze with wide-open eyes, to see something remarkable, **to see beyond the natural.**

Our spiritual eyesight is more important than anything, just as the eagles eyesight is to the eagle; he could not survive without his amazing eyesight. Similarly, we need our spiritual eyesight to be sharpened and it will benefit us to be teachable and learn from the eagle. **The key is discovered when we see where the eagle abides and how his eyes work:**

1. The eagle abides on the high inaccessible rock on the cliff:

It is from the high places on rock that he spies out the prey! Only In Christ Jesus, when we are born again and filled with the Spirit, does our spiritual eyesight come to life. Then the eyes of our heart are awakened as Paul prayed:

Ephesians 1: 18 *"That the Father of Glory may grant you a spirit of wisdom and revelation, of **insight** into the mysteries and secrets in the deep and intimate knowledge of Him, **by having the eyes of your heart flooded with light**."* This is how we

73

"**see beyond**" the natural into the supernatural realm of God.

The eagle has incredible eyesight.....from as far up as 3 miles he can see a small rabbit in a field of corn, or from the same distance he can clearly see a salmon swimming upstream in rough white water. No other bird has anything like this eyesight and this is why the Bible says,

Job 39:29 *"He spies out his prey from afar off."* The higher he goes, the wider his vision, so with us. The closer we abide in the Lord, the more He will be able to reveal to us! The Bible illustrates that in many scriptures, here is one example:

1 Corinthians 2:9-11 *"Eye has not seen and ear has not heard ....all that God has prepared for those who love Him...yet to us God has unveiled and revealed them by the Spirit, for the Holy Spirit searches diligently, exploring and examining everything, even the bottomless things of God.....no one discerns [comes to know and comprehend] the thoughts of God except the Spirit of God."* We, too, must depend on the Holy Spirit as Jesus did in every aspect of His life, then we shall "see beyond" as He did.

John 15:4 Jesus said: *"Dwell in Me and I will dwell in you, live in Me and I will live in you."* Where we live opens up our spiritual vision, just as the eagle spies out his prey from afar as he lives up on the rock.

From the beginning of Creation, God spoke by the Spirit to Adam and Eve:

Genesis 2: 29 God said: *"See!"* What was man to see? He was to **"see beyond"** the natural, to see into the eternal or literally **"To see as God sees!"** God said: *"I have given you......plants, trees, the animals..."* In other words, Gods sees BEFORE, then He speaks and everything comes into being by the spoken Word of God. That was how it was always meant to be for man....**to see as God sees**, then to speak it into being!

It was this supernatural ability to "see beyond" that was one of the things Satan attacked:

Genesis 3: 5 *"In the day that you eat of it your eyes will be opened, and you will be like God."* This was the deception by Satan. Adam and Eve already were like God, made in His image and they could already "see beyond," so what was God meaning when He said in:

Genesis 2: 17 *"Do not eat of the fruit of the tree of the knowledge of good and evil;"* God had planned to preserve and protect this special gift of "seeing beyond," so that mankind would always "see as God sees." They would be free to see and choose God's ability, not to be limited by only using their own natural vision.

Here we see Satan at his most cunning; how he set out to pervert this special gift God had given [he couldn't take it away] so he wanted to distort it with evil. He was only successful because Adam and Eve did not appreciate or value what God had given to them. We see the result:

Genesis 3: 6 *"The woman saw...."* This word is 'Ra'ah'....the carnal way of seeing from a selfish point of view that relies on what is natural and not eternal. From this time on, mankind has only had the natural ability to see with distorted human vision. Occasionally we see in the Old Testament that there are some instances where the Spirit of God intervenes and opens spiritual eyes for a specific purpose. This happened when Elisha prayed for his servant's eyes to be opened:

2 Kings 6: 17 *"Lord I pray You, open his eyes that he may see. And the Lord opened the young man's eyes and he saw and behold, the mountain was full of horses and chariots of fire round about Elisha."* To be able to 'see beyond' depends on **God** and that is one of the things that the Messiah came to do! It was prophesied many times such as:

Isaiah 42: 7 *"To open the eyes of the blind, to bring out prisoners from the dungeon and those who sit in darkness."*

The Messiah, Jesus Christ, would come **to restore** what had been stolen....to **"See beyond."**

Luke 11: 34 Jesus, Himself said: *"The eye is the lamp of the body."* Paul said:

1 Corinthians 2:12 *"Now we have not received the spirit that belongs to the world, but the Holy Spirit Who is from God, given to us that we might realize and appreciate the gifts of divine favour and blessing so freely and lavishly bestowed on us by God."* **v 14** *"But the natural man does not accept the revelations of the Spirit; he is incapable of seeing them because they are spiritually discerned."*

All the way through the New Testament we see that supernatural insight is restored as the Spirit comes. John, the beloved, on the island of Patmos, spoke in the letter to Laodicea: **Revelations 3: 18** *"Purchase from me salve to put on your eyes that you may see."* Here is the "Seeing beyond" again….the supernatural vision of the Spirit. John tells us in **Revelations 1: 10** *"I was in the Spirit rapt in His power on the Lord's Day."* It was while John was in the Spirit, that God opened up to him all the spiritual revelation of the book of Revelations…John was "seeing beyond." It is where we dwell that is the key for this supernatural "Seeing beyond."

2. <u>The eagle has eyesight that cannot be distracted:</u>

Once the eagle sees his prey, **his eyes never leave it.** He has an amazing ability to concentrate and focus because he has "set" not only his wings, but his desire!

2 Corinthians 4: 18 Paul said: *"Since we consider and look not to the things that are seen, but to the things that are unseen….the things that are invisible are deathless and everlasting."* We as Christians, IN Christ, need to "set" our vision and not be distracted as we learn from the eagle.

Hebrews 12:2 NIV *"Let us FIX our eyes on Jesus, the author and perfecter of our faith, Who for the joy set before Him endured the cross……."* The word "fix" is a very active word, so we need to decide to be a "doer" of the word then we shall "See beyond" the natural!

76

1 Corinthians 9: 24-26 *"So, run your race that you may lay hold of the prize and make it yours......do not run uncertainly without definite aim."* It has often been said that if you aim at nothing you will hit the target every time! Every one of us needs a vision; we need short-term and long-term goals to live as victorious people in Christ.

Philippians 3: 14 Paul again made it so clear - *"I press on toward the goal to win the prize."*

It is important to remember that whatever we focus on we will reflect. We are called to be mirrors that brightly reflect Jesus.

2 Corinthians 3: 18 *"All of us with unveiled face continued to behold ["see beyond"] in the word of God, as in a mirror the glory of the Lord; are constantly being transfigured into His very own image in ever increasing splendour and from one degree of glory to another; for this comes from the Lord Who is the Spirit."* What we think most about...that is where our focus is...and that is what we will reflect!

3. <u>The eagle's eyesight depends on a special solution:</u>

When an eaglet is born, there is a special soft solution at the back of his eye, which hardens as he grows. This forms like a built-in compass set to "home," just as a real compass is always set to "north." This means that the eagle can always find its way back to the nest, no matter how far away he may have flown. What happens is that as he might go the wrong way, he begins to experience a low level pain at the back of his eyes that communicates that he is off course. We too, when we are born again, have been given spiritual compasses to keep us on course and we would be foolish to ignore them! These are some of the signs.......

a) Loss of peace:

John 14:27 Jesus said, *"Peace I leave with you; My peace I now give to you."*

Colossians 3: 15 *"Let the peace, soul harmony which comes* *from Christ rule, act as an umpire continually in your hearts, deciding and settling with finality all the questions that arise in your minds."* If you lose your peace, something is wrong...STOP and seek the Lord immediately!

Isaiah 9: 6 *"He is the Prince of Peace."*

Psalm 119: 165 *"Great peace have they who love your law; nothing shall offend them or make them stumble."* If, for instance, you find yourself getting offended and lose your peace, then it is a sure sign you are way off course in living as Christ would have us live! It is danger time.....Taking offence is when you have grieved and quenched God, Holy Spirit and are going in the wrong direction! TURN around in true repentance and go "home" like the eagle.

b] Loss of Joy:

Psalm 16: 11 *"In Your Presence is fullness of joy."*

Isaiah 12: 3 *"With joy you shall draw water from the wells of salvation."*

Nehemiah 8: 10 *"The joy of the Lord is our strength."* Joy is our inheritance in Christ Jesus so when our joy has gone then something is radically wrong!

John 15: 11 Jesus said, *"That My joy and delight may be in you."* When we have lost our joy, we are weak and certainly need to heed our spiritual compass as soon as possible.

c] Feeling that you are being controlled by others:

Beware of taking other peoples priorities and burdens on board. Jesus said: **Matthew 11: 29-30** *"Take My yoke upon you...for My yoke is easy."*

We need to flow in our own anointing; do what you have been called to do, do what grips your heart, not what someone else thinks!

Zechariah 4: 6 *"Not by might nor by power but by My Spirit, says the Lord."* "See beyond" and keep on track as you respond to your own spiritual compass like the eagle.

4. __The eagle is born with eyes that rotate 180%:__

The only way the eagle's eyes can do this, is that they are activated by a daily oily solution. This is released from the back of his eyes to lubricate the eye ball to give the eagle this remarkable ability! "Seeing beyond" with our spiritual eyes is dependent on our closeness and fellowship with the Holy Spirit from the very day we are born again, it is a gift we need to cultivate.

Acts 6: 4 *"Devote yourselves steadfastly to prayer and the ministry of the Word."*

1 John 1: 3 *"What we have seen [see beyond] and heard, we are also telling you, so that you too may realize and enjoy fellowship....with the Father and with His Son Jesus Christ."* I believe that it is what we SEE in the spiritual realm, when in close fellowship with the Lord, that enables us to have anything to share at all. For myself, as a preacher, it is these precious revelations that become life to me and then become the essence of a message that will in turn bring life to others. Enjoy the sweet intimate fellowship with the Holy Spirit, it is your "Manna from heaven" so that you can see as God sees!

2 Corinthians 13: 14 *"The fellowship, communion and sharing together and participation in the Holy Spirit."*

Let us be people who are not just walking in the Spirit, but live a life prompted by the Spirit. Simeon and Anna are good examples, who came to the Temple just at the right time, when the parents of Jesus brought in the Child Jesus.

Luke 2: 27 *"Simeon prompted by the Holy Spirit came to the Temple...he took Him up in his arms.....Now I have* ***seen*** *[seeing beyond] your salvation."* How did Simeon see the difference between one baby and another? The Spirit of the Living God had opened his eyes to SEE the real Jesus, even hidden in a baby's body.....Amazing!!!!

Romans 8: 14 *"For all who are led by the Spirit of God are sons of God."*

5. **The eagle must keep his eyes free from all dust and impurities:**

We too, may need to allow the Holy Spirit to prune away things that would hurt our vision.

John 15: 2 Jesus said, *"My Father is the Gardner....He cuts away and He cleanses and repeatedly prunes every branch that continues to bear fruit to make it bear more and richer fruit."* It would be so wise for us to let go of the superfluous, then the Father will be able to refine what we are called to do. We may even need to allow the Holy Spirit to bring closure to things in our lives that are good, but not necessarily the best for us in the new season...Always He has only the best plan for us to be more and more fruitful. Pruning can be painful, but so necessary as I have had to learn!

One example of God pruning me many years ago may help to explain what I really mean. I knew my calling to preach, I was frustrated because I couldn't see it happening which is not a good place to SEE what God is doing! In what seemed to be a miraculous way, I found myself elected as president of the local Aglow Chapter. I was excited and was busy thanking the Lord the next day when the Holy Spirit suddenly quickened a scripture to me **2 Samuel 6:7** *"God smote him there for touching the ark."* Without warning the "fear of the Lord" came upon me and I sensed strongly that if I took this position I would die spiritually. I want to make it clear that it was nothing to do with Aglow, it was simply not what God had planned for me at that time. As you can guess, I struggled with this, discussed it with Skippy, but in the end it was my obedience that counted to the Spirit of the Lord.

The Father was definitely refining my life and it was painful. As I only wanted to be obedient, I quickly resigned but the outcome was that no one could understand and that meant that I did not have an easy time! However, it has been amazing that some 20 years later I find myself ministering in many wonderful Aglow Chapters! What was that all about? The Holy Spirit has revealed some truths, but mainly I believe it was God looking for my responsiveness to whatever He said. Delayed obedience is disobedience and will spoil our vision quicker than anything else!

Remember, **it is not us that do this**...the Father is the Gardener; we just respond and relax, stop struggling and embrace His best for our lives. However, we do need to do the important things that God says to do...and then we shall be stress free. Obedience is the pathway to blessing and then His unlimited Grace abounds to us in a miraculous way!

John 5: 30 Jesus said: *"I am able to do nothing from Myself, but only as I am taught by God....I do not seek or consult My own will, but only the will and pleasure of the Father Who sent Me."* Pleasing the Father should be our highest priority every day.

1 Thessalonians 2: 4 *"Not to please men, but to please God."*

Colossians 1: 10 *"That you may walk in a manner worthy of the Lord, fully pleasing to Him and desiring to please Him in all things, bearing fruit in every good work and steadily growing **and ever increasing in......clearer insight**."* "Seeing beyond" is closely linked to fruit bearing to the Glory of God.

Recently I was at a Conference with a well known Bible teacher and he was exhorting us to "See beyond." He referred to this as the ability **to see on the inside of us** ...a picture, a word or an image in our imagination like a spiritual womb conceiving and then bringing something supernatural to birth.

Hebrews 11:1 *"Faith perceiving as real fact what is not revealed to the senses."*

"Seeing beyond" is a faith walk; it is seeing as real, what is not yet perceived with our natural eyes, it really is supernatural eyesight!

2 Corinthians 5: 7 *"For we walk by faith and not by sight."*

Hebrews 11: 6 *"Without faith it is impossible to please God."*

I personally deeply responded to this message and on the last night of the Conference, I was totally taken unawares.... **I began to "see beyond" the natural!** There was an enormous angel standing several feet directly above and behind the preacher. I could see the angel's hand on his heart and from the hand were streams of light, power and fire going into his heart as he was preaching. At the same time in his other hand was a big sparkling jewel encrusted sword, this seemed to be being wielded back and forth to protect his back and his mind while he was delivering the Word. This angel was so big and real to me....my eyes on the inside of me were "seeing beyond" and it was absolutely amazing. Everything else dimmed into insignificance! I have a strong feeling that as you are reading this the Holy Spirit is stirring up a longing inside you to "see beyond" into the supernatural realm, if that is so....Please pray this prayer and expect it to happen!

Father God I come in the Name of Jesus Christ and ask You Holy Spirit to put salve on my spiritual eyes, and open them to "See beyond" as it is written in Your Word. Thank You Father.

We need eagle eye sight to "see beyond," to allow the Spirit to open up the heavens and enable us **to live a life "prompted by the Spirit"** in our day to day lives so that we can "Dare to be an Eagle!

Chapter Eight
ON EAGLES WINGS

"The way of an eagle in the air"
Proverbs 30:19

This is all about the lifestyle of the eagle. The Bible says: "It is too wonderful." **Exodus 19:4** *"How I bore you on eagles wings."*

The wings of the eagle have a wing span of between 7-8 feet.....massive, strong and flexible and made up of literally hundreds and hundreds of small hidden feathers, each one vital, yet most of them unseen. Then there are also the hundreds of larger, stronger and very handsome main feathers. These form the frame of the two wing structures. The wings of the eagle are so complex, yet so simple; every part working in synchronization, moving in harmony to pick up the slightest gust of wind to soar that bit higher. The eagle goes highest when he has to go over the storm as the mighty "ruach" winds lift him up on rushing hot air currents. He ascends to unbelievable heights, using the very winds that destroy things on the ground to carry him over the fury of the storm to safety on the other side. The eagle goes so high that he will be covered with ice, his head, his wings, every part of him; the weight of the ice causes him to descend on the backside of the storm. Who knows, if it were not for the ice, maybe he might just keep going and never come down!

The Divine Eagle carries us, as the mother eagle carries her young. Every tilt of the wings, every adjustment of the wing feathers all working for good at the eagles command; changing, lifting and spreading and acting for speed as he swoops down, or acting as a "break" to slow him down so he doesn't have a crash landing. So similar for us: **Romans 8: 28** *"All things work together for good for those who love God and are called according to His design or purpose."* God does it for the eagle, how much more will He do it for us who love Him! The design is perfect for the wings, so also His design is perfect for our lives! Everything the eagle needs for life and survival is found in the perfect creation of his wings. So for us too, the Bible says:

2 Peter 1: 3 *"His divine power has given us everything we need for life and godliness through our knowledge of Him Who called us, by and, to His own glory."* Yet still, to be successful, the eagle needs all his other attributes......for example, his amazing eye sight is paramount and so are the sharp talons and the beak, but most of all he needs his incredible intelligence and personality. The wings may do the carrying but essentially it is **everything that he is that makes the eagle king of all the birds**. We have so much more to learn from him if we are willing and teachable.

1. The wings of the eagle give him **BALANCE** and we need to walk in a balanced way. Excess is dangerous and is an open door to enemy action in our lives:

Ecclesiastes 7: 18 *"The man who fears God will avoid all extremes."* The eagle moves his wings subtly, keeping in balance all the time with no exaggerated movements that could endanger his life. For us we need to be sure that:

Hebrews 4:11 *"We strive diligently to enter that rest of God."* Stop "flapping" like a chicken! Ask the Holy Spirit to make you a person of balance!

Remember, how we behave should reflect Jesus to those around us.

John 14: 9 Jesus said, *"Anyone who has seen Me has seen the Father."* The character we exhibit will either draw people to Jesus or repel them. They should see Peace and Joy, His Kindness, His Goodness, His Mercy and His unconditional Love, Graciousness and our countenance should always be shining!

2 Corinthians 9: 8 *"God is able to make all grace abound to* *you in abundance."* People are watching us to see how we handle the hard times.....they deserve to see the real Jesus in us even when we are going through those difficult circumstances.

I remember my dear friend and prayer partner during the last few months of her life. She battled a horrific form of cancer, but never did she question or even once speak anything except that she was healed.....that was what she believed! Every time I or anyone else was with her, we were uplifted, encouraged and made to feel special. She overflowed in supernatural peace, joy and love and always imparted these to others....her countenance reflecting more of Jesus each day as she drew nearer to Him. Even in the difficult periods of Chemotherapy, she was flying on eagles wings...no crash landings for precious Ruth! Then one day, she soared right up into His Presence, almost physically lifting her own spiritual wings and "seeing beyond" she went to be with her Beloved Lord. **Balance comes from the Spirit within, and it is such an inspiring quality**....just like the eagle!

2. The eagle is the most LOYAL and disciplined of all birds and he mates for life...this is what he was created for! We would do well to imitate this loyalty; disloyalty leads to betrayal, as it did for Judas. Speak to the Lord about how loyal you are and pray that the Holy Spirit will guard you from all disloyalty in Jesus' Name.

1 Corinthians 4: 16 Paul could say, *"I implore you, be imitators of me."* Can we say this too? Help us Lord!

Some behaviour of the eagle is inbred, while other behaviour has to be learnt along the way. For instance, he gains in expertise how to hunt and kill his prey. However, the eagle soars alone, or with their mate, they are not like other birds that fly in flocks. That is why sometimes there can be a tendency to feel alone....When this happens, don't fight it, enjoy it because it is the spiritual eagle inside us that goes higher and further than many others. Be careful of the company you keep!

1 Corinthians 15: 33 *"Do not be deceived or misled! Evil companionships corrupt good character."*

3. The eagle is DEVOTED to his mate and shows this especially during the time of incubation. He will fly to her with "flowering twigs"...almost like a bouquet of flowers presented by an earnest husband! In fact, he will even pick up bright objects such as bottle tops, shiny things or even pieces of silver foil for the expected eaglets......you could say, he brings "toys" for his children. The eagle is not only attentive to his mate, but he is a devoted father sharing responsibility for sitting on the eggs and also for feeding the young eaglets when they arrive. Pray to the Father that He will guide you into a life of complete devotion to bring Him Glory.

4. How we walk in the Spirit, how we use our spiritual wings can clearly be seen in how we RELATE TO OTHERS...... to our spouse and children and it really does matter! We should be the "best" husband/wife, the "best" possible mother/father, grandparents, and the "best" possible child to our parents. That honours the Lord! It is nothing to do with how they have treated us, or are treating us, however badly! We should be doing everything "as unto the Lord!" That is our responsibility.

Matthew 25: 40 Jesus said, *"Whatsoever you do to the least, you do to Me."*

Let's follow the example of the eagle! God has placed us in our family, they are not perfect...but neither are we! As many preachers have said, "The biggest room in the world is the room for improvement!" Make this your heart cry and see the Holy Spirit answer.....O Lord, I need Your help to notice, to praise, to appreciate and value my family, please be my "Helper" day by day as I can not do this without You. Amen.

Make sure it is not in a religious or legalistic way because this causes division not harmony. We need to bring Christ into the centre of our family....demonstrating unconditional love, loyalty and faithfulness. Decide to be available when they need help, after all Christ is there for us! No, we do not put our family relationships above God, nor do we allow the family to dominate or control our lives....its all about **"balance"**. It is all about priorities, being in God's order; it is about the "heart,"...learning to be Christ-like in our families and to lay down our lives for others.

5. Being like Jesus in our GIVING OF OURSELVES to others:

John 10: 15 Jesus said, *"I am giving My own life and laying it down on behalf of My sheep."*

John 15: 13 Jesus said again, *"No one has greater love than to lay down his life for his friends."* Simply cry out to the Holy Spirit in prayer.....Lord Jesus, make me more like you in giving of myself to bless others. Amen

We do have spiritual wings and we should be using them. The Bible says: **Isaiah 40:31** *"They shall lift up their wings and mount up close to God as eagles...."* Our Spiritual wings are not just for us to soar above, as we saw earlier, but they are **TO CARRY OTHERS**, just like the mother eagle. She does not carry the young all the time, she has a specific purpose. Her motive is to move them on from the boundaries of their comfort zone, out of the nest! In fact, she even uses her wings to nudge and push the young eaglet forward to the very edge of the nest before actually tipping it over! God, as our Divine Eagle certainly does this with us. Both God, as the Divine Eagle and the mother eagle are much more interested in destiny...than in us, or her young eaglets, feeling comfortable!

I believe that **God uses the wings of other people** in our lives to nudge us forward towards our destiny. Sometimes we do not appreciate all that is happening at the time, but looking back we can see the hand of God in a situation and the great benefit that it has brought to us.

In removing all the soft furnishings of the nest, the mother eagle is definitely making things very uncomfortable for her young as the thorns stick in! It reminds me of Paul: **2 Corinthians 12: 7** *"There was given to me a thorn in the flesh."* None of us know for certain what exactly that thorn was, but it was "in his flesh", not his spirit! Could it be that God was using someone's wings to nudge Paul forward, to keep him from being puffed up and proud? I do not know for sure, but I find it interesting that the young eaglet, when he begins to feel the discomfort of the sharp thorns sticking into him, he puffs up his feathers to try and cushion himself but nothing works.....**the mother eagle has a mission** to get him to the edge of the nest, and out of it and flying! However, the young eaglet is always very reluctant to move towards the edge. The great unknown beyond the comfort of the nest does not appeal to him at all!

It is good to learn spiritual truths from every avenue available to us, even from the young eagle. We should never resist moving forward and be very careful not to struggle against the wings of other people. We need to keep moving forward in our Christian journey, make sure that our spirit is sweet, no matter what happens, never losing sight of soaring above as we flow in the power of God. Being "airborne" and loving it, is our destiny!

So when does the mother eagle carry her young? There is only one occasion....when they are learning to fly! The loud fearful screech reaches her ears, as the young eagle falls helplessly towards the earth.....Immediately she goes into action and swoops down at about 200mph and picks him up on her spread-out powerful wings. The principle is the same for us, The Divine Eagle hears our slightest cry, even the cry of the heart and comes to our aid and carries us on His wings.

Hebrews 2: 18 *"He, Himself, He is able to run to the cry of those who are being tested."* But the Divine Eagle does not intend us to be carried for long.....we too need to fly! Similarly, the mother eagle only rescues her young eagle so that she will once again take him high up into the sky before tossing him off her wings repeatedly, UNTIL he has learnt to use his own wings and fly!

Imagine for a moment, if you can, how the young eagle felt. "Wow! That was a close thing! Oh thank you Mama for picking me up, thank goodness I am safe now; what a great view from up here on your wings, this is the easy life, just going up, up and up; it's wonderful Mama, you are doing all of the work! This is so much better than being in the nest...I will forget all about the nasty falling sensation...I am free, I am safe on your wings Mama"........ BUT NOT FOR LONG! The mother eagle has a different purpose for her little eagle; he must fly....whatever it takes! So with no comforting, no indulging, no warning she flips him off; once more he is falling......again he cries, "Why, why did she do it to me? I thought she loved me, why doesn't she care?"

Does this sound familiar? Could this be our attitude when unexpected things happen? Be sure that the wings that hold and carry us can also nudge us off to greater heights! This must be a time when we need to be sure to keep our attitudes right with everyone, especially towards God Himself. Oh, the mother eagle watches, she is always ready to rescue him again and again if it is needed; but this process will be repeated until the young eaglet opens his own wings and discovers he, himself, can fly. Her motive is a higher motive....he has to fly! The eagle has been created for freedom; he has to be free! We, too, as people of the Spirit, like the eagle, have been created for freedom, this is our calling. **Galatians 5:13** *"For you, brethren, were called to freedom."*

There is a time in our growth towards maturity when God will actually allow us to come to a place where we may "feel" as if we are falling. Yes, we may even scream and complain and maybe "feel" abandoned; but all the time The Divine Eagle is watching. Sometimes we may have damaged our spiritual wings or even have a broken wing and if necessary, He will swoop down and carry us on His wings until we are able to use our own spiritual wings. If that has spoken to you please don't go on until you have prayed......Lord Jesus, thank You that You know and understand what it is like to have a broken wing, as You died on the cross. Please bring me healing and restoration by the power of Your Holy Spirit so that I will once again be able to use my spiritual wings and fly above all the circumstances. Amen.

God's purpose is for us always to fly towards our destiny.... our comfort is not His main priority! Then again, there can be a situation and God will use another person to pick us up on their wings. The Lord of Glory knows what is best in every particular instance......Just trust Him!

Let me explain; as human beings we like our lives to be smooth sailing, peaceful and easy, we don't like the turbulence when we feel out of control. But God, has a different agenda and wants us to exercise our spiritual wings of authority and learn to resist the devil. Jesus defeated the last enemy at the cross, but we have to establish His victories in our day to day lives...using our spiritual wings and wielding the two-edged sword...the Word of God. This is all part of our spiritual journey!

Inside every Believer, is the "Breaker Anointing" which comes in seed form, as does as every other gift and characteristic of Christ. This is our spiritual DNA. It must be developed and learned how to best use it, first in our own lives, and eventually for the good of others. We need to start saying "No" to the enemy, let The Breaker Himself rise up in us and bring "breakthrough" to us and our situations:

Micah 2: 13 *"The Breaker, the Messiah will go up before them. They will break through, pass in through the gate and go out through it, and their King will pass on before them, the LORD at their head."* Our spiritual wings are not only to enable us to fly, but to help others to fly. Pray that the Father Himself, will bring you to the place where you too will be able to "carry" others in their rough times.

During my Christian journey, these spiritual wings have begun to be developed to help others. For the last few years God has given me the privilege of being a "mother in Israel" to many younger women. I often push them out of their comfort zone so that they will begin to use their own spiritual wings and learn to fly in their own anointing. Each year we have a Day Conference "Woman without Limits" and my aim is to release young eaglets - these very special young women and to see them soar on eagles wings. I am sure if you asked them, very often they feel distinctly uncomfortable, inadequate and weak....but that's OK...as long as it doesn't stop them launching into new territories for Jesus. Then comes the joy unspeakable, as they spread their wings......The Holy Spirit sends the supernatural wind and they discover what it is to soar into the unlimited horizons of their own unique anointing. I love it! I love to see them fly, to see their wings, at first hesitatingly open, then the sheer delight as they begin to use their own spiritual wings and ascend higher than they ever dreamed possible! God is SO faithful, He loves to use us...No wonder The Divine Eagle thrills when He sees us fly towards our destiny. This is what we have always been created for....**to fly on eagles wings!**

Chapter Nine

STIRRING UP THE NEST

"As an eagle that stirs up her nest"
Deuteronomy 32:11

After several weeks of tender loving care, the mother eagle suddenly changes her behaviour. She knows it is now time for her young eaglets to leave the nest and learn to fly, as we have seen in the previous chapters. How she prepares for this is equally important to us in learning to fly and to continue being able to soar above all the storms that life may throw our way. The mother eagle reaches down into the nest; she rips out the feathers, breaks up the twigs and overturns their nice comfortable home.

We see how God, as the Divine Eagle, allowed this to happen as the pressures built up leading to the departure of the children of Israel from Egypt. **Exodus 2:23-24** *"After a long time the king of Egypt died, the Israelites were groaning because of the bondage. They kept crying, and their cry because of slavery ascended to God."*
Exodus 5:7 *"You shall no more give the people straw to make brick; let them go and gather straw for themselves."* **v9** *"Let heavier work be laid upon them."* Sometimes things can seem to get worse before they get better, but always remember, God knows what He is doing and He is in full control! God had spoken to Moses, right at the beginning that He would harden Pharaoh's heart. Then we read of all the plagues and miracles and how the terrible circumstances eventually motivated the Israelites to be ready to leave for the promised land. Many times our discomforts, sorrows and disappointments have become nests that have been overturned to put us on the "cutting edge" and launch us out

into ministry. I know I would not be where I am today if God had not overturned my life many times and permitted me to walk through the deepest darkness in order to find myself on the "cutting edge" flying in the Spirit!

Perhaps one of the greatest illustrations is found in the Book of Esther:

Esther 2: 6-7 *"Mordecai…who had been carried away from Jerusalem, and brought into exile…he brought up his orphaned niece Hadassah, that is Esther, and took her as his own daughter."* Wonderful! Now this beautiful and lovely orphaned child has a place called home, a family and comfort for the first time in her life…..a nest where she is safe, loved, cared for, fathered and accepted. But then:

Esther 2: 8 *"The king commanded all the young beautiful maidens to be taken into the royal harem, and Esther was taken into custody."* The Divine Eagle was certainly allowed to "stir up her nest"….but God, once again, had a higher motive than her comfort…He had a destiny for Esther to use her "spiritual wings" and carry her nation to safety.

How did she cope in the hard place of the harem? We are told that she went into the custody of Hegai, the king's chamberlain. Could this be the Holy Spirit hidden in the Old Testament? I believe that Hegai represents the Holy Spirit and He was commissioned by God to look after Esther, even in the harem, to see that she would be supervised and prepared to fulfil her destiny as the Queen. So we surely see how Esther gains favour even in the dark places of the royal harem. Whenever our nests are stirred up, I am convinced that God will provide everything we need in the Holy Spirit.

John 16: 17 Jesus said, *"I am telling you nothing but the truth when I say it is profitable, good, expedient, advantageous for you that I go away. Because if I do not go away, the Comforter, the Counsellor, the Helper, the Advocate, The Intercessor, The Strengthener, The Standby will not come to you; but if I go away, I will send Him to you to be in close fellowship with you."* Esther experienced this truth in a prophetic way, as she was brought to the kingdom for "such a time as this." Yet follow her story and we find again later on she had to be prepared to leave a different nest. This time it was a nest of rules, regulations and court protocol as she sought an audience with the king that could result even in her death. What a "cutting edge" for Esther as she decided to spread her spiritual wings:

Esther 4:16 *"I will go to the king, though it is against the law; and if I perish, I perish."* **Esther certainly found her nest stirred up**, but we know that the Holy Spirit came with the incredible winds of such favour, wisdom and divine grace that she was eventually used to save her people from destruction. Right choices, at a time when the nest is stirred, will propel you quickly towards your destiny!

I believe it would be helpful if we looked at some of the nests that The Divine Eagle will surely want to stir up in our lives:

1. **Materialism.**

Our relationship to material things is a vital issue.

1 Timothy 6: 10 *"For the love of money is the root of all evils."* It is what we crave for and desire that is evil, money of itself is not evil, rather it is neutral and it depends how we use it...whether it is for good or for evil. We all need to put our earthly possessions completely at God's disposal. This is why my ministry "Cutting Edge" is committed to "New Hope for Africa", an orphanage and school for almost 400 homeless orphans in Kampala in Uganda. I am constantly reminded how the eagle gives to his mate and gives to his young eaglets. We too, would do well to move out of this nest, this false sense of security, this comfort zone of materialism and begin to give in an unlimited way.

Matthew 6: 33 Jesus said, *"Seek first His Kingdom and His righteousness and then all these things that your Heavenly Father knows well you need......will be given to you besides."* This really is an issue of the heart; no-one forces the eagle to give, it's in his DNA. Our spiritual DNA is seen when we use our spiritual wings to give to others too and fly the nest of materialism. Let us Pray:

Show me Lord where I am relying on the things of this world, I want to fly the nest of materialism in Jesus' Name. Amen.

2. **Spiritual Complacency.**

This may seem a warm and comfortable nest, but it will mean that you live your life far below the best. Never fulfiling what God has planned for you will make our wonderful Heavenly Father so sad and I am sure none of us want to do that. How much better is it to expand your spiritual wings, take a risk and launch out into the new horizons towards your fullest potential? The Divine Eagle has one desire to get us out of the nest of complacency, and up into the air. The Good Shepherd came not merely to give us life, but to give it more abundantly:

John 10: 10 Jesus said, *"I came that they may have and enjoy life, and have it in abundance."* Some of us may spiritually live too close to the world and wonder why we do not experience the abundance that Jesus promised? We need to beware of being complacent about our salvation and wary of having our faith in the things of this world, instead of storing up riches in heaven where moth and rust do not corrupt:

Matthew 6: 20-21 *"For where your treasure is, there will your heart be also."* We are called to a life of adventure in the Holy Spirit, free from all that would keep us bound to the nest.

One excellent example is to be found in **Judges 5:17** *"Asher sat still by the seaboard clinging to his creeks."* Although this is a different metaphor from the nest to the creek, the principle is the same. There was Asher sitting by the sea board, clinging to his creeks, when he could have launched out into the ocean and experienced the joy of great adventure.

95

Do not settle for the comfort of the known when The Divine Eagle is wooing us out of the nest into greater heights and the freedom that we were created for. Let us discover the hidden treasures of God's untapped gifts within us and respond to His nudge and spread our spiritual wings to leave the nest and fly! Let us Pray:

O Father, I don't want to settle for less than Your best, teach me Your ways and help me to fan into flame all the gifts You have given me so that there is no complacency in my life. Amen.

3. **Guilt, Inferiorities and Inadequacy.**

These are spiritual nests which we can grow accustomed to. If we stay there long enough, they will eventually imprison us and we will begin to hate ourselves. That is when the nest becomes a place of masks, of pretence and unreality...looking alright on the outside but on the inside, there is a spiritual serpent hiding in us and eating away at our faith. How do I know? I have been there. The key for leaving these nests is to allow God, The Divine Eagle, to reveal how He accepts us unconditionally in His Son, The Lord Jesus Christ: **Ephesians 1:** 7 *"I am accepted in the Beloved."* We need to respond as He nudges us in His love and compassion towards our new freedom, accepting ourselves as we trust Him never to let us go. Instead of frantically striving on the inside then we will come to a place of peace. A chicken flaps but the eagle soars! Yes we can make mistakes; we do miss the mark and sin, but whatever happens..... MOVE ON and don't settle back into those nests. God will discipline us, but His discipline is never in anger, always in love and always for our best. He is a good God! As spiritual eagles, we must fly using our spiritual wings. Just as The Divine Eagle shows mercy to us in love, nudging us to move beyond the confines of these nests, so we need to adopt the same attitude towards ourselves and others and go for it. It has been said, by someone, of the Holy Spirit that: "He comes not only to comfort the afflicted, but to afflict the comfortable!" Whatever is your particular limitation is pray that the Holy Spirit will lift it out of your life as you respond in prayer and take time in His Presence:

O Lord God Almighty, all of my life I have felt guilty,[inferior or inadequate] I know it has been something that the enemy has been able to use time and time again. Now I repent and ask You to forgive me and wash me in Jesus' blood so that I can really move on and not be limited by these same negative things. Thank You Lord. Amen.

4. **Negativity.**

This nest may not seem a comfortable place at first glance, but if we believe the negative words and actions long enough, especially those that have been said to us, or about us, by people we love; then that nest becomes a barrier to our destiny. In fact we often use negative things as an excuse for not being adventurous and stepping out into new things with God. The Holy Spirit will bring us to the very edge of this nest and in loving confrontation He will enable us to leave this nest behind and go forward.

Let me give you an example of a beautiful young woman, we will call her Denise. She came for help after one of the Conferences; she desperately wanted to please God and fulfil her destiny, but realized that there was some hidden barrier. As Denise and I sought the help of the Holy Spirit, He revealed that her mother and, more particularly, her father, whom she deeply loved, had always said crushing negative words over her life ever since she could remember. So much so, that Denise believed these words to be true and they had become part of what she accepted about herself. Sayings such as: "You will never be any good." "People will laugh at you, so don't try." "You don't have the ability of your brother." "You are timid and shy and don't worry about it, we like you that way."......I think you get the picture! Denise's parents had no idea they were damaging their daughter, they loved her and just wanted to protect her. However, these words over the years were like arrows with poisoned heads that the enemy used to penetrate her spirit over and over again. On the outside Denise was a successful, "got-it-together," young woman, everyone would have thought of her as a spiritual eagle but inside there was a chicken hiding. In fact there was a nest that badly needed to be overturned; if she was to fulfil her destiny. The Divine Eagle worked so beautifully. Denise forgave her parents, forgave herself for accepting the negative words and she took back the ground that the devil had stolen. The nest of negativity had had to be stirred up and overturned, the Lord, Himself, brought her to the edge of the nest and later it became her launching pad into a new unlimited life in the Spirit. You can do this too as you pray!

5. **Fears.**

This nest is made up of lots of big branches, twigs and then covered over with the so called soft stuff. Yes, just like the eagles nest, it is built on the high places of enemy action usually during the years of childhood and it will hold us back from ever flying beyond the circles of our own fears. It is a nest of self-destruction and more limiting than any other nest.... we must seek our freedom. If I share a little of my testimony, you will understand how fears are added on top of one another to build a fortress around our lives, often giving us a false sense of security that keeps us imprisoned in the nest.

When I was five years old in rebellion, I did not listen to my parents and this always opens the door for the devil. My parents had told me to wait until they could check the second-hand bike that I had been given but I went ahead and took it out and it resulted in a very nasty accident as the brakes did not work. I went over the handle bars and my glasses caused a deep cut over my eye which needed a great many stitches. In those days it was customary to administer Chloroform on a large pad over the face. I remember the absolute terror, of screaming and struggling as I felt they were smothering me. Many years later, the Holy Spirit stirred the nest of my fears and revealed that that incident was the root of all my fears. Of course from then on the enemy made sure he built on those fears with more and more instances of fear until it became a stronghold in my life. Isn't it interesting that the eagles nest is called a stronghold in: **Job 39: 28** *"On the cliff he dwells and remains securely, upon the point of the rock and the stronghold."* The nest of fear is built up as the devil floods fearful situations into our lives bit by bit, especially when we are vulnerable as children. Some fears are totally irrational, but none the less have to be confronted in the love of God. **1 John 4: 18** *"There is no fear in love, dread does not exist, but perfect love turns fear out of doors."* Love, God's love, is the answer to all our fears.

The Divine Eagle is: *"The Altogether lovely One."* **Song of Songs 5: 16** *"This is my Beloved, yes He is altogether lovely."* It is not our love for Him that will get rid of our fears, but God's love for us. Just as the mother eagle loves her eaglets and does not push them out in anger or frustration, neither does our Divine Eagle do anything, except out of His incredible love for us.

God's perfect love for us will bring us to the edge of these "strongholds of fear," because God wants us free, He will nudge us in love, beyond the prison of this nest. **To be free we need to:**

a] Recognise the fear

b] Realize that we have given in to fear by not trusting God's love

c] Repent for our fearful response

d] Renounce, out loud, all fear in Jesus Name

e] Replace the fears by using our authority and **command** all fear to leave and not come back

f] Present the ground of these fears to the Holy Spirit and ask Him to fill you with God's amazing love **Romans 5: 5** *"For God's love has been poured out in our lives by the Holy Spirit, Who has been given to us."*

g] Finally be prepared to "do it anyway" even in fear....and the enemy has no common ground in you! If you still have difficulty, get a mature person to stand with you and as you agree together and go through these steps you will be able to leave the nest of fears once and for all.
Luke 4:18 Jesus said, *"He has sent Me to announce release to the captives..."*

There are many other nests that The Divine Eagle will stir up to bring us into the freedom that Jesus won for us on the cross at Calvary.   One that I would like to mention specifically is the nest of:

6. Rejection.

This so easily becomes a stronghold and most people have experienced and suffered rejection at some time in their lives. However, I know that The Divine Eagle, in His love for us will stir up this nest so that we begin to hate the false comfort that it gives us. Rejection happens, that is a fact. More often than not it is not our fault, but it is our responsibility how we respond.   Staying in this nest means shutting ourselves in, withdrawing and putting up barriers so that others can't reach us. The result is we begin to live in a "stronghold or walled city" that ends up as a prison of self-protection from more hurt. For God to break up this nest of rejection, we need to find out the root and deal with it, much the same as we deal with our fears.

For myself, after several years of choosing time and time again to forgive those who had rejected me, I sensed in The Holy Spirit that I needed to find the source of the infiltration. Sure enough, He showed me that when my mother was pregnant with me, she desperately did not want to bring a child into the world, in a place like London, when Britain was at war. I will always be eternally grateful that she did not decide to abort me; but it was this rejection that deeply affected me, even as an unborn baby. At times like this, is when the enemy sows evil seeds which were planted by the devil when I had no way of defending myself. Then, as life went on, again and again instances would happen, so that over and over again those seeds were watered by various incidents and the seeds of rejection sprouted and produced bad fruit in my life.

But now, even after several years, my testimony is that God has set me free from this vile nest of rejection that Satan used to use so often to try and limit me. Freedom was only possible by God's acceptance and love, with His victory and power, with His patience and grace.....Yes now I can say that if the Holy Spirit can do it for me then He can do it for you! Dare to be an eagle, decide that you will not be kept in the nest of rejection anymore. Make a choice that you will not live in the prison of "fearing rejection from others." The following Scriptures are truths that will help break you free as you seek personally the Lord God Almighty as your wonderful Deliverer. Pray with all your heart in the Name and Power of Jesus Christ to bring you into freedom from all rejection.

John 8:31-32 Jesus said, *"You shall know the Truth and the Truth will set you free."*

Romans 8:31 *"If God is for us, who can be against us?"* Jesus came to set the captives free as I have said before.

Lastly , whatever you do, **do not fall into the trap and start rejecting yourself,** this is exactly what the devil wants and you need to resist that at all costs! The answer lies in BELIEVING the Word of God, CONFESSING the Word of God and PRAYING IN the Word of God.

Romans 8:35-39 *"Who shall ever separate us from Christ's love? Shall suffering and affliction and tribulation? Or calamity and distress? Or persecution or hunger or destitution or peril or sword? [or rejection?].....* **Yet amid all these things we are more than conquerors and gain a surpassing victory through Him Who loved us.** *For I am persuaded beyond doubt that neither death nor life, nor angels nor principalities...nor anything in all creation will be able to separate us from the love of God which is in Christ Jesus our Lord."*

Chapter Ten

HOVERING AND OVERSHADOWING

"Hide me in the shadow of your wings"
Psalm 17.8

Psalm 91: 1 *"He who dwells in the secret place of the Most High, shall remain stable and fixed under the shadow of the Almighty, whose power no foe can withstand."*
    The eagle hovers over his young, he hovers over his prey, he hovers over waste land and then he sees.....**Job 39: 29** *"His eyes see it afar off."* When the eagle sees he goes into action, whether it is to defend his young eaglets, to swoop for his prey or spy a storm brewing in the distance; whatever he sees while hovering affects his movements afterwards.

1. The first time we see the word **"HOVERING"** is in:
Genesis 1: 2 *"The Spirit of God was hovering, moving, brooding over the face of the waters."* The Bible says: *"The earth was without form and an empty waste and darkness was upon the face of the very great deep;"* but God saw "potential" in all the nothingness and darkness. Isn't that just so encouraging? When He looks at us, no matter what might seem to be dark, chaotic or empty, God sees potential for His Kingdom purposes; not because of how we are, but because of His ability! In this portion of scripture we see in:
Genesis 1:2 *" The Spirit of God was moving [hovering, brooding] over the face of the waters."*
Genesis 1:3 *"And **God said!**"*...... When the Spirit and God's Word come together....THEN there is creation!
Webster's Dictionary says: To hover is 'to be suspended over', 'watchfully poised' and 'to maintain altitude without moving forward' i.e. "a state of readiness."
    In the beginning, The Spirit of God was poised

watchfully, ready to go into action as soon as the Word was spoken. Many people, for instance, do not seem to understand why we need to confess with our mouth that we are saved. It is because of the power of our confession that God, the Holy Spirit, can hover over the words and bring to pass the miracle of salvation.

Romans 10:10 *"For with the heart a person believes and with the mouth he confesses his salvation."*

The eagle hovering is a picture of the Holy Spirit Who is watchfully waiting all the time to work in our lives according to what we speak. If we speak God's Word, then the Spirit is ready to create and activate what we speak....if we speak negatively as I have already said, then the enemy of our souls is ready to bring that to pass.

Proverbs 18: 21 *"Death and life are in the power of the tongue, and they who indulge in it shall eat the fruit of it for death or for life."* That is an awesome scripture and we need to remember that the Spirit of God is hovering just as He did in the beginning and has to wait for the "spoken" word from our lips; but so is the enemy of our souls. So be careful! God's Word is God's will, God's Word is His purpose......as we agree in harmony and speak out the Word of God, then the Holy Spirit broods over it and breathes life into the spoken word and creation happens in us and through us.

Faith jumped into my heart a long time ago, when I realized just how I could work together with the Holy Spirit and see God's plan and purposes fulfiled and potential realized. It was this revelation which changed my life and brought the Kingdom of God into a new dimension. Again and again I have seen the Holy Spirit brood over a word and bring it to pass. This was quite amazing in the case of a particular young, rebellious teenager, who we will call Russell......he had so many problems and I realized that only Jesus could change him. The Lord showed me how to confess a scripture over him with thanksgiving:

2 Corinthians 5: 17 *"Father, I thank You, in the Name of Jesus and in the power of The Holy Spirit that Russell is a new creation, the old has gone and the new has come."* I confessed this word over and over again each day as the Holy Spirit quickened it to me......and just six months later, to the day, it happened. He was born again and truly the word of God was created in him. Not always does it happen so suddenly and dramatically...sometimes we need to persevere but it will happen! The Spirit of God hovers over God's Word and creation happens. Let us learn from the eagle. He represents the Holy Spirit and it is the Holy Spirit Who is watchfully poised, hovering over our lives, just waiting to hear the Word of God on our lips so that He can bring it to pass. He desires to bring life to the waste places, to defend us, to change us, to pull out all the hidden potential in our lives that He can already see so clearly; even as He is hovering over us right now.

2. "OVERSHADOWING"......

Time and time again, we are exhorted in the Bible to hide under the shadow of His wings....to remain there, to dwell there; we are told that it is a safe place under the shadow of the Almighty. Let us see how the eagle "overshadows" his young eaglets and learn from him. The eagle hovers and as he hovers, he stretches out his enormous wings and these form an even bigger shadow over his young. Do you perhaps remember playing "shadow games" when you were small, how the shadow was so much bigger and sometimes even made you afraid? The actual shadow that the wings of the eagle form does just this; they are magnified and form a shadow of protection, a covering to his young brood. I am told that there is always one of the eagle parents that overshadow above the nest as they continue to grow in the nest. The young eaglets live under the shadow of Papa/Mama's wings and they are kept safe. At the same time this creates a "longing" in each of the young eaglets, that one day, they themselves will rise nearer to the sun.....to be like the fully grown eagle and have wings that produce such large shadows!

So with us, we should abide under the shadow of the Almighty, know His protection and covering; at the same time have an ever-increasing longing to get closer to the Son of Righteousness himself:

Malachi 4:2 *"To you, who fear My name, shall the sun of righteousness arise with healing in His wings."*

The wings of the eagle reflect God's unlimited Grace....the riches of His free grace toward us in Christ Jesus. Everything we have is all by grace; it is the gift of God because He first loved us while we were sinners.

Romans 5: 8 *"God shows and clearly proves His own love for us by the fact that while we were sinners, Christ died for us."* As Charles Wesley's great hymn says so powerfully, "Amazing Grace, how can it be that Thou my God should die for me?" This truth is clearly seen in this scripture:

2 Corinthians 5: 19 *"It was God in Christ, reconciling and restoring the world to Himself."*

HOW DID IT ALL BEGIN?

Luke 1:35 *"The Holy Spirit will come upon you and the power of the Most High will* **overshadow** *you like a shining cloud."* The angel Gabriel spoke those words to Mary in answer to her question: "How can it be?" The angel had just told her that she would become pregnant and give birth to a Son, Jesus the Son of the Most High..... Absolutely impossible in the natural, so God decided to do the supernatural by "overshadowing her!" **v37** *"For with God, nothing is impossible and no word from God shall be without power."* The answer was in the "overshadowing" by the Holy Spirit Who would come upon her and she would be "overshadowed" by the power of God. Quite amazing!

Let us look at the word "OVERSHADOW."

Webster's Dictionary says: to tower over, to shade, to serve and tend, to envelope in a haze of brilliancy and to make an investment.

I found the last meaning so illuminating. When you "make an investment in something," you are putting some of your resources into something that you hope will become bigger and give you a good return for your investment. Now look at this "overshadowing" in a new way. God is doing the investing into Mary as she is "overshadowed" by the Holy Spirit. He is putting His own Seed of His own Beloved Son into the womb of a young girl called Mary, so that she can give birth and bring forth The Saviour of all mankind. The Redeemer Himself, was being invested into Mary as she is "overshadowed by the Holy Spirit and the power of God! Quite staggering! Can you now see how the eagle teaches us? The meaning of the word shows us that it also means: to cast a shadow, to oversee, to protect, and to provide a shelter. God, as The Divine Eagle was looking for a shelter, a place for His investment, where He could spread out His wings and overshadow the growing Son of God Himself. The Overshadowing by The Most High will always create a total dependency on Him; it will always bring an investment into our lives from on high from The Spirit of God. You could say: "an overshadowing" is a vital impartation and a life-giving encounter with the Living God that will leave a deposit in us for eternity!

In every account of the Transfiguration, when Jesus took Peter, James and John up the high mountain and he was transfigured before them and there was an overshadowing. **Matthew 17:5** *"A shining cloud overshadowed them."* **Mark 9:7** *"A cloud threw a shadow upon them."* Whenever there was an "overshadowing" in the Bible there was a purpose of impartation....an investment was going to be made. So what happened here at the Transfiguration? God was affirming His Son: A voice said, *"This is My Son, My*

Beloved Son, with Whom I am, and always have been, delighted. Listen to Him." Just before this "overshadowing," the Disciples had seen Elijah and Moses with Jesus.....but afterwards **v8** *"they saw only Jesus"* The investment that God Almighty was making in this "overshadowing" was a new unparalleled revelation of Jesus, The Personhood of Christ Himself, His incomparable greatness as The Only Begotten Son of God and that there are no equals to Him. I believe that as they were "overshadowed," it can be seen as "enveloped in a haze of brilliancy."

Colossians 1: 27 *"Christ in me the hope of Glory."*

When the eagle overshadows his young, he is investing in them a picture, a reflection, a hope, a glimpse of what they will become......the wings of protection, of covering as the eagle "towers" over the young eaglets, "tending and serving" them as the word "overshadow means.

So with us, The Divine Eagle overshadows us with the picture of Christ in all His Glory and Majesty, seated above, enthroned on high.....how He watches, defends, shelters and covers us at all times. Christ Himself, "towers" way, way, beyond us. Our God is enthroned beyond and above all earthly limitations as Isaiah saw prophetically all those years before Christ actually came.

Isaiah 40:22 *"It is God Who sits above the circle of the earth....."*

1 Corinthians 15: 26 *"He has defeated the last enemy....Death is swallowed up in victory."* In this uncertain time we live in, we so desperately need a new vision of the magnitude and magnificence of our great God and at the same time where He has placed us beside Him in the heavenly sphere in Christ Jesus.

Ephesians 2: 6 *"He has raised us up together with Him and made us sit down with Him in the heavenly sphere in Christ Jesus."*

How incredible that it all began as the Holy Spirit "overshadowed" Mary! Now, The Divine Eagle wants to "hover and overshadow" you and me, to continue investing more and more of Himself in us.......so that we grow up to reflect His beauty and His character as we dwell in the shadow of His wings.

Perhaps you would like to ask the Holy Spirit to overshadow you? If so, do pray with me.......

Heavenly Father, I am so grateful that You have invested the immortal Seed of Your Son, the Lord Jesus Christ, in me on that day when I was born again. Please will You "overshadow" me with Your Holy Presence and Power and give me a new vision of the greatness of Your Godhead so that I can behold more and more of Your eternal goodness and Your Glory.... Amen.

Chapter Eleven

MOUNT UP CLOSE TO GOD

"They shall mount up close to God as eagles mount up to the sun"
Isaiah 40:31

Webster's Dictionary: "To Mount up" means......To wing upward, to soar toward the eternal, to make a steep ascent, to climb to higher levels, to reach upward, to move upward, to rise, to grow, to advance, to launch upward, to move upward, to attain greater height or magnitude, to be equipped to rise to another level.

Strong's Concordance: "Mount up" comes from the Hebrew word, "Alah" which means, to ascend, to arise, to climb up, to shoot forth, to spring up or to excel.

The Legacy of the eagle, is to pass on to its off-spring everything of his innate ability and to develop all the inbred DNA to the fullest possible potential. The fully grown eagle has one desire for the young eaglet; that it will eventually take his/her place as a fully mature eagle created to be king of all the birds. The eagle does this for example in his customs, behaviour and all his ways: **Proverbs 30: 29** *"This is too wonderful!"*

I see exactly the same principle with The Lord Jesus Christ, Messiah, Saviour and Redeemer, Who came to give us new birth. Jesus perfectly demonstrated how we could live and walk in the Spirit of God here on earth and how we could follow in His footsteps. How then later when He had returned to the Father, He personally sent God the Blessed Holy Spirit to come and indwell us.

John 16: 17 Jesus said, *"It is profitable for you that I go away. Because if I do not go away, the Comforter, Counsellor, Helper, Advocate, Intercessor, Strengthener, Standby.... The Holy Spirit* *will not come to you; but if I do go away, I will send Him to you to be in close fellowship with you."* This is how we have the power within us to fulfil our destiny and mount up as eagles close to God:

Ephesians 1: 19 *"So that you can know and understand what is the immeasurable and unlimited and surpassing greatness of His power IN and FOR us who believe...."*

I believe it will be helpful to see from the Word how this applies to us:

Romans 8: 14 *"For all who are led by the Spirit of God are sons of God."*

Romans 8: 15-16 *"You have received the Spirit of adoption, The Spirit producing sonship . The Spirit, Himself, testifies together with our own spirit that we are children of God."* You may have heard that many years ago, Charles Wesley would always ask people "do you have the WITNESS of the Spirit?" Today you might hear people say, "I know in my "knower" deep inside me." The point is that no person can give you assurance of salvation; it comes from the Spirit within. From time to time you may feel the need of extra assurance. This is when we stand on the Word of God. The Bible says that: "the infallible Word of God will never fade or pass away."

Romans 8: 17 *"We are heirs of God and fellow heirs of Christ and we enjoy the first fruits of The Holy Spirit....a foretaste of the blissful things to come."*

John 14:16-18 Jesus Himself said of the Holy Spirit, *"He will remain with you for ever...He will be in you....I will not leave you as orphans....I will come back to you."*

I have come to love the eagle more and more and I will never cease to marvel how God has used him so vividly in the Bible, how the eagle teaches us, exhorts us and inspires us to live the Spirit-filled life to the Glory of God. Now, with the help of the Lord, I want to encourage you to mount up close to God and to rise to another level; to experience personally a new dimension in Christ Jesus. This was Paul's heart cry:

Philippians 3: 10 *"For my determined purpose is that I may know Him, that I may progressively become more deeply and intimately acquainted with Him, perceiving and recognizing and understanding the wonders of His Person more strongly and more clearly, and to know the power out-flowing from His resurrection."* Here we can see that it is clearly a very godly desire to flow in the anointing of the Holy Spirit and that there is always more! Coming to know the Holy Spirit as a Person is the only way that this will happen, and He is always ready to help us.

Isaiah 40: 31: *"You shall run and not grow weary, walk and not become tired."* Too often I see many struggling Christians, tired and weary and all they need to do is mount up close to God and "Dare to be an Eagle."

I am sure that very often you will have heard preachers speak about the time of the 'new level' or the 'new dimension' and your spirit leaps in hope and longing, but then you are left wondering: how is this going to be possible for you? Is that true?

My heart's desire is that you will be able to mount up close to God and experience this personally, not just once, but as a principle to LIVE in another dimension. Desperation will not take you to another level, but hunger has a part to play as it fuels our desires, [sometimes for the wrong things!] but handled positively, hunger is a good starting place as to how to mount up close to God. If you are still with me this far in the book, I guess you are still hungry!

To mount up close to God you need to have:
1. HUNGER:
John 6: 48 Jesus said, *"I am the Bread of life."*
John 6: 63 *"The words that I have been speaking to you are spirit and life."*
Even in the Old Testament:
Deuteronomy 8: 3 *"Man lives by every word that proceeds out*

112

of the mouth of the Lord." Jesus Himself quoted this in His confrontation with the devil in the wilderness.

Isaiah 40: 8 *"The Word of our God will stand forever."*

In the New Testament:

2 Timothy 3: 16-17 [NLT] *"All scripture is inspired by God and is useful to teach us what is true and to make us aware of what is wrong in our lives. It straightens us out and teaches us to do what is right. It is God's way of preparing us in every way, fully equipped for every good thing God wants us to do."*

I have been told that in a certain primitive tribe in South America, the mothers rub the inside of a special root constantly around the mouth of their small infants just after they are born, long before they can eat solids. What happens is that they lick off the flavoured substance, smell it, taste it and begin to crave for it. This root later on, will become their main staple diet and is essential to their growth and well-being. The mother knows that she needs to create this hunger in her young child. So we need to become more and more hungry and feed on the Word of life.

You also need to confess His Word over your life, your family and all situations...it is a wonderful way to learn Scripture. Remember there is power in His Word!

2. EVER INCREASING FAITH:

Romans 10: 17 *"Faith comes from hearing and hearing by the Word of God."* So we see again that the Word of God is crucial to our faith.

Hebrews 11: 6 *"Without faith it is impossible to please God."*

Galatians 5: 6 [NLT] *"What is important, is faith expressed through love."*

To have an ever-increasing faith it can be very profitable to read about the men and women of faith in the Bible .Imagine yourself in their positions, slip into their skins and begin to understand how they felt, what they went through and how they had to trust in the Holy Spirit and how they

113

stepped out in faith. One of my favourite characters hidden in the New Testament is found in **Luke 13:11-17** *"There was a woman there who for eighteen years had had an infirmity caused by a spirit, a demon of sickness. She was bent completely forward and utterly unable to straighten herself up or to look upward. And Jesus saw her......"* Why do I love this woman so much? Because that could have been me:

For forty years I was unable to straighten up, on the inside I was crippled, twisted, even though I went week by week to church just like the woman did; nothing changed UNTIL one day Jesus saw me! Yes it was her special day and how I can relate to this tormented woman! Oh hallelujah, Jesus notices whatever has been dumped on us to make us bowed down, He sees our disabilities, whether they are spiritual or bodily and His word makes the difference.....It is still the same today; Jesus said to her, *"Woman, you are loosed from your infirmity. Then he laid His hands on her and instantly she was made straight and she recognized and thanked and praised God."* Even as I write to-day I can remember the miracle of that day in my life as if it was only yesterday, such is the power of the Word of God!

Another character that I especially love is Sarah, who had to wait so long for her promise.
Hebrews 11:11 *"Because of faith also Sarah herself received physical power to conceive a child, even when she was long past the age for it, because she considered God Who had given her the promise to be reliable and trustworthy and true to His word."*
Hebrews 11:39 *"All of these won divine approval."* If you want to win divine approval, read and re-read about these real people who came through all their difficulties in faith.

Read books about men and women of faith in our own world over the generations....if they could do the amazing things they did, so can you! God says you do have a portion of faith.
Romans 12: 3 *"Each according to the degree of faith apportioned*

by God to him." All you need is faith as big as a mustard seed. **Matthew 17: 20** Jesus said, *"I say to you, if you have faith that is living like a grain of mustard seed, you can say to this mountain...Move from here to yonder place, and it will move; nothing is impossible to you."* I love the true story of young Christian orphaned children during a time of Revival in the Far East a few years ago, who just believed they could speak to the mountain and it would be removed. They were facing losing their home because of mountain subsidence, so together they believed and prayed in the Holy Spirit and quite literally enormous bulldozers and earth-moving machines were brought in and moved the mountain! They believed for a miracle and they saw a miracle!

Matthew 18:3 Jesus said, *"Truly, I say to you, unless you repent and become as little children, you can never enter the kingdom of heaven."*

Be with people of faith, it rubs off. Become part of a faith-filled church that preaches the Word without compromise.....that will spur you on in your walk of faith.

2 Corinthians 5: 7 *"We walk by faith not by sight."* Exercise your faith, like muscles it grows with training. Don't allow fear to hold you back in your faith walk.

3. MORE LOVE:

1 Corinthians 13: 13 *"The greatest of these is love."*

John 15: 10 Jesus said, *"Abide in My love and live in it, just as I have obeyed My Father's commandment and live in His love."*

Luke 10: 27 *"You must love the Lord your God with all your heart and with all your strength and with all your mind; and your neighbour as yourself."*

2 Corinthians 5:14 Paul said, *"The love of God constrains me."* That was the bottom line for Paul, this was his reason for everything he did!

Perhaps like me, you may feel that there are times when you just don't seem to have enough of God's unconditional love? I am so grateful that God knew that you and I would need it, so He sent the Holy Spirit to give it to us! I am realizing that I have repeated this Scripture time and time again, I make no apologies, this is how we get God's love.....it is His gift to us from the Holy Spirit!

Romans 5: 5 *"For God's love has been poured into our hearts by the Holy Spirit Who has been given to us."* I believe that it is only God's love that will draw us and enable us to mount up close to God. I have found that whenever I focus on my love for Jesus, it is possible for my love to fluctuate and this can leave me in an unstable or vulnerable position. However, when I am focused on Christ's love for me...that is a very different thing.... I am secure in His unconditional love which is always the same from everlasting to everlasting.

Jeremiah 31: 3 *"Yes, I have loved you with an everlasting love; therefore with loving-kindness have I drawn you and continued My faithfulness to you."*

Isaiah 43: 1 *"He Who created you says....I have called you by name; you are Mine."* All these truths will build you up as you are filled with His Spirit and you will begin to flow in His amazing love more and more.

Another way is to dwell on the wonderful **Psalm 139** and allow the Spirit to show you how precious you are to Him. Every verse is full of treasures to encourage you, such as: **v13** *"For You did form my inward parts; You did knit me together in my mother's womb."* **v17** *"How precious and weighty also are Your thoughts to me O God! How vast is the sum of them!"* Now begin to believe His Word and mount up close to God, worship and adore Him as you marvel at His love and tenderness for you. I can promise you that no one else loves you like He does!

4.   SEEK THE LORD AND EXPLORE HIS CHARACTER IN HIS WORD:

Nahum 1: 7 *"The Lord is good, a Strength and Stronghold in* *the day of trouble; He knows those who take refuge in Him."* One of the most important things to always remember is that **God is always good and He has always got the best for you** ....nothing can change this! Sometimes, we may think He is not fair, that is because we only see from a human, limited perspective; **He is always just and faithful.** Mount up close to God, as the eagle mounts up close to the sun and have a new vision of His faithfulness!

2 Timothy 2: 13 *"If we are faithless and do not believe and are untrue to Him, He remains true and faithful to His Word and His righteous character, for He cannot deny Himself."*

Hebrews 13: 8 *"Jesus Christ is the same, yesterday, today and forever."*

Hebrews 13: 5 *"I will not, I will not, I will not in any way leave you helpless nor forsake you, nor let you down nor relax My hold on you! Assuredly not!"* When God says this, he means it! No one else has ever shown such love or faithfulness to you or me....nor will there ever be anyone to compare with Him. He is yearning over us right now with an eternal longing and passion to embrace you and me . Don't make Him wait any longer for your sweet fellowship.....mount up close to God!

5. PREPARE YOURSELF:

Joshua 1: 11 Joshua said to the people, *"Prepare!"*

Joshua 3: 5 *"Sanctify yourselves for tomorrow The Lord will do wonders among you."* We do have a part to play, as we have seen how the eagle prepares himself; but we need to remember that we now have the Holy Spirit and He will cleanse us from all sin and draw us to Himself with the Blood of Jesus Christ. In His presence it is imperative that we respond to whatever He shows us....DO NOT STRIVE! David is a good example to us, as we see how he has come through the hard times to mount up close to God. **Psalm 139: 23-24** *"Search me, O God, know my heart; test me and know my thoughts. Point out anything in me that offends you, and* *lead me along the path of everlasting life."* Be courageous, "Dare to be an Eagle" and pray this prayer and it will change your life!

Psalm 73: 28 *"But it is good for me to draw near to God."*

Acts 13: 22 *"I have found David a man after My own heart."* David knew the immeasurable treasure to be found in the Presence of the Lord.

Psalm 17: 15 [NLT] *"As for me, my contentment is not in wealth but in seeing You and knowing all is well between us."* That is the peace that passes all understanding, how grateful we should be that:

Ephesians 2: 14 *"Jesus has broken down the wall of hostility, now we can go right into His Presence!"*

Matthew 27: 51 *"The veil has been torn from top to bottom."* The way is now open into the most holy place; we don't need a priest, as they did in the Old Testament. We do not need Mary or anyone else to intercede for us, we don't need a special format of a prayer or any special robes....we just come simply by faith in the Lord Jesus Christ, trusting in His blood to take us right into the Presence of God. Oh what an incredible Saviour!

Hebrews 4: 16 *"Now we have free access to come boldly to the very throne of God."* As I dwell on these amazing scriptures I am overwhelmed with thanks giving that it is possible for us to mount up close to God.

6. MAKE GODLY CHOICES:

You are what you choose to be! You can be as far away or as near as you desire to God. Jesus cried out "It is finished!" You CAN mount up close to God.

I remember one of my first journey's to minister abroad was to Jamaica and as I set out to prepare myself and the word, suddenly the heavens seemed as brass. I was excited, felt privileged and wanted so much to honour the Holy Spirit but what was I to do? I already had the word for all the Conferences that I was booked to do.....FREEDOM...but I was experiencing no freedom in my preparation. I made a choice and decided just to read and read the Word of God aloud and believe that the Holy Spirit would be working the Word into my spirit. I chose to continue doing this for a week, then another week until I had completed four weeks with no obvious difference. I had decided that I would press into the new level that must be waiting for me. It was a choice to mount up close to God. All I can tell you is that God honours our Godly choices and He is no mans debtor. When I started to minister He began to release a special new powerful anointing as soon as I started to preach. I had walked into a new dimension by my choices and saw the Holy Spirit bring freedom to all the people who were hungry wherever I went. Hallelujah!

There is power in the choices you make. Never underestimate the power in small choices; they are not insignificant and they do matter. Most of our lives are more affected by a series of small Godly choices, it is seldom that you will mount up close to God by one big choice...much more likely it will happen as you decide to regularly choose God's way and be obedient to what He says.

7. GRACE AND PEACE:

Romans 1: 7 *"Be yours from God our Father and from the Lord Jesus Christ."* As we humble ourselves before God something amazing happens:

James 4: 6 *"He gives us more and more grace, the power of the Holy Spirit....* **but** *God sets Himself against the proud, but gives grace continually to the lowly, those humble enough to receive it."* I believe to rise to another level - to actually mount up close to God, to move upward towards our destiny is a mystery. Let me explain...I have found that the way up is down! Perhaps John the Baptist discovered it all those years ago when he said, speaking of Jesus, the Lamb of God:

John 3: 30 *"He must increase and I must decrease."* How does this work in our everyday lives?

Quite often I am asked, "Do you get nervous or anxious before you share?" I used to speak all the positive words that I knew were right, but which were not exactly true.... until a few years ago! Truly, the more I have gone on in my Christian journey, the more inadequate I have felt. I have discovered that in my carnal nature I am less and less self-assured; whereas in my spirit-man I have become more and more confident in Him and His ability and anointing in me. This did not make sense until I was sharing at a Conference with a very special lady Heather Double; many will remember her with such affection and gratitude as I do. God has used her, as well as others, to spur me on to write this book. She would always say to every new venture, "Course you can!" On this particular occasion we were sharing about some of our vulnerable places, I opened up how I was concerned that I was feeling more and more inadequate when going to minister; Heather listened and then agreed to pray for me. I will never forget her prayer.....it shook me to the core of my being and my life was forever changed. It went something like this – "Thank you Lord for the doors you have opened up to Gill, thank you Lord for her obedience and willingness to go through them; now Lord increase her dependency on You, increase her own inadequacy so that she will only be confident in You. Amen." That prayer was not what I expected, but it was certainly what I needed. I am eternally grateful to this "mother in the Lord" for her wisdom, counsel and encouragement that have been so often invaluable in my life.

1 Corinthians 15: 10 Paul said, *"I am what I am by the grace of God and His grace toward me was not found to be without effect."*

To mount up close to God you need His unmerited grace and favour ALL the time. Remind yourself of the eagle and you will not forget that it is His spread out wings that reflect the abounding grace of the Lord God Almighty. It is by grace alone that we mount up close to God.

2 Corinthians 9: 8 *"And God is able to make all grace come to you in abundance."* **v11** *"So you will be enriched in all things and in every way."* **v14** *"All because of the surpassing measure of God's grace in you."*

I have tried to give you "rungs on the ladder," or perhaps "stepping stones" would be a better metaphor, so that you can, without fail "mount up close to God." This is our ultimate destiny, to be close to God:

James 4: 8 *"Draw close to Him and He will draw close to you."* Jesus gave His life so that you and I could know Him in an intimate, close and personal way. Complete salvation is being able to be intimate with God, the Holy Spirit, that He will be your very best friend; that He is the closest Person to you, more real than even your spouse, children and ministry. You were created for God's pleasure. He loves you and wants to show you how much He loves you, so you can then say, I love You too.

Mount up close to God and discover that eternal life is all about knowing God intimately. When you are intimate with God, He's blessed and you are changed and transformed. You are infused with stability and strength, instead of falling apart at the slightest thing. You boldly mount up close to God and enjoy His Presence and then you, **"Dare to be an Eagle"**.

Conclusion

BE AN EAGLE

As I said at the beginning of this book, "Dare to be an Eagle" was God's idea." It was born in my spirit-man very unexpectedly and quite supernaturally. Thank you for sharing my journey, the ups and downs; but please do not lose the nuggets of gold that may have spoken to you personally from these pages. I do most sincerely pray that "Dare to be an Eagle" will have both challenged and inspired you to live your Christian life as an eagle, and not like a chicken! If you discover yourself entangled or trapped on the Rock...remember that your Heavenly Father has already sent the Holy Spirit to come and bring you the freedom that Jesus won on the cross for you. The eagle in you has to be free, whatever you do, make a positive choice not to succumb passively to the traps of the enemy.

Isaiah 40: 31 *"Wait for the Lord, expect, look for, and hope in Him.*

Isaiah 30: 18 *"The Lord earnestly waits, expecting, looking, longing to be gracious to you; and therefore He lifts Himself up, that He may have mercy on you and show loving-kindness to you. For the Lord is a God of justice. Blessed are all those who earnestly wait for Him, who expect and look and long for Him...for His victory, His joy, His matchless unbroken companionship!"*

Isaiah 40:31 *"Mount up close to God as eagles mount up close to the sun; run and not be weary, walk and not faint or become tired."* Let the Holy Spirit put new wind in your sails.

This is my heart-felt prayer for you; you are so special and I love you too, even though I may not have met you personally, this book is for you and comes with the everlasting love of God! May you, my dear unknown friend, have the unparalleled experience of "soaring" with God, the Holy Spirit into the new dimensions He has for you in the corridors of heaven and brush your spiritual wings against the face of God.

This is my prayer for you.......

Father God, I thank You so much that You have demonstrated Your unconditional love by sending Your only Begotten Son Jesus Christ to die on the cross as the perfect sacrifice. Lord Jesus I marvel at Your love in giving everything, even Your life, so that no one might need to perish but have everlasting life. Holy Spirit I honour You, as Jehovah "Shammah" You are God with us, I am entrusting into Your hands this very special child, Father, that You will have met them in a very personal, unique and powerful way as they have read this book. O Lord please will You keep Your hand of power on them and impart the supernatural courage and inspiration that they need to "Dare to be an Eagle" and give You all the Glory. Amen.

Acts 20: 32 *"And now I commit you to God, I deposit you into His charge, entrusting you to His protection and care. [He is The Divine Eagle perfect in every way] And I commend you to the Word of His grace.....He is able to build you up and give you your rightful inheritance."*

I sincerely pray that as The Lord grants you even more revelations about the eagle, and I am sure He will, that you will share these to encourage, comfort and inspire others to: "Dare to be an Eagle."

PRAYER OF SALVATION

Father God in Heaven I acknowledge that I am a sinner and that I have fallen short of Your righteous standard. I deserve to be judged for eternity for my sin. Thank you for not leaving me in this mess, for I believe you sent Jesus Christ, Your only begotten Son, who was born of the Virgin Mary, to die for me and carry my judgement on the cross. I believe He was raised again on the third day and He is now seated at Your right hand as my Lord and Saviour. So on this day..................... I give my life entirely to the Lordship of Jesus. I believe Jesus is the Son of God. Lord Jesus I confess you as my Lord and Saviour. Please come into my life through your Holy Spirit and change me into a child of God. I renounce the things of darkness and all sin – wash me in the blood of your Son Jesus Christ. From this day forward I will no longer live to please myself but live to please You who gave Yourself for me that I may have the gift of eternal life and live forever.

I thank you Lord Jesus; my life is now completely in Your hands. I receive a new heart and a right spirit as I put my trust in you and know you are so merciful to me. Thank you again dear Lord.
Amen.

PRAYER TO BE FILLED WITH THE HOLY SPIRIT

Father, in the name of Jesus Christ, I come to you as Your child. You said if I asked You for the Holy Spirit, You would give Him to me. With joy and gratitude for all you have done, I now ask in faith. Please baptize and fill me at this moment with your Holy Spirit. I receive all you have for me as I surrender all that I am and have to You. You promised to give me ability and power when the Holy Spirit comes upon me, including the release to speak in tongues, my love language just for you. So now in faith, I receive and speak in new tongues to glorify You my Lord and Master.
Amen

INTRODUCING Gill Gifford and CUTTING EDGE

Since Gill's dramatic salvation experience on Boxing Day 1979, when she died and went to heaven.....and God sent her back to work for Him! Subsequently she went to Bible School training under the excellent supervision of Colin Urquhart and the late Bob Gordon, she has, along with her husband Skip, been in leadership in different places in UK, and had six years of leading an English Church in Mallorca in Spain, where they still live. Gill has been married for thirty three years to Skip, they have two children and five grandchildren.

Cutting Edge Ministries was born as a result of much encouragement from those benefiting from a number of Conferences. For ten years she regularly led seminars for Rachel Hickson at "Heartcry" Conferences across UK and Northern Ireland. Gill now travels more as an Apostle, doing Conferences in many parts of the world. For the last five years she has hosted her own "Cutting Edge" Conference each year and also hosts a day Conference, "Woman without Limits." Gill has a deep passion to encourage people to live out the Word of God fully and freely, operating in the Holy Spirit and reaching their full potential and destiny in Christ to the Glory of God.

Why "Cutting Edge"? Because so often lives have been wounded, damaged and hurt by the cutting edge of people's words, the past and traumatic situations; while others have been pierced, crushed or stabbed by the circumstances of life. In fact, everyone has been on the cutting edge! But Jesus came to, *"heal the broken hearted, to proclaim liberty to the physical and spiritual captives and the opening of the prison and the eyes to those who are bound."* To proclaim, "This is the Year of His favour." **Isaiah 61: 1-2**

The sailing boat represents the true cutting edge of the Spirit-filled life of freedom, excitement, progress and purpose, leaning into God in total dependency on Him. It means cutting the moorings that hold us, launching out all in God and allowing the Spirit to take us out on the great swelling tide of His plans and purposes. It means leaving behind the smooth waters just inside the harbour, moving out into the great unsearchable riches of Christ to fulfil your spiritual destiny, letting down the nets into deep waters, soaring beyond and Daring to be an Eagle. This certainly is the most exciting and fulfiling time to live in and we must make a difference, because it is SO close to Jesus coming back again!

Website: www.gillcuttingedge.org
www.youtube.com   access through gillcuttingedge